MICHAEL   DANNY   MICHELLE
KEATON   **DeVITO**   **PFEIFFER**

BATMAN
RETURNS

WARNER BROS. PRESENTS

A TIM BURTON FILM MICHAEL KEATON

DANNY DeVITO MICHELLE PFEIFFER "BATMAN RETURNS" AND CHRISTOPHER WALKEN

MICHAEL GOUGH PAT HINGLE MICHAEL MURPHY MUSIC BY DANNY ELFMAN CO-PRODUCER LARRY FRANCO

EXECUTIVE PRODUCERS JON PETERS, PETER GUBER, BENJAMIN MELNIKER, MICHAEL USLAN

BASED UPON BATMAN CHARACTERS CREATED BY BOB KANE AND PUBLISHED BY DC COMICS STORY BY DANIEL WATERS AND SAM HAMM

SCREENPLAY BY DANIEL WATERS PRODUCED BY DENISE DI NOVI TIM BURTON DIRECTED BY TIM BURTON   WB

BATMAN™
RETURNS

**NOVELIZATION BY CRAIG SHAW GARDNER
STORY BY DANIEL WATERS AND SAM HAMM
SCREENPLAY BY DANIEL WATERS**

WARNER BOOKS

A Time Warner Company

WARNER BOOKS EDITION

Copyright © 1992 DC Comics Inc.
All rights reserved. The stories, characters, and incidents featured in this publication are entirely fictional. All characters, their distinctive likenesses, and all related indicia are trademarks of DC Comics Inc.

Cover photo courtesy of Warner Bros.

Warner Books, Inc.
1271 Avenue of the Americas
New York, NY 10020

W A Time Warner Company

Printed in the United States of America

First Printing: July, 1992

10 9 8 7 6 5 4 3 2 1

BATMAN™
RETURNS

PROLOGUE

Gotham City isn't safe anymore. It's crowded, noisy, dirty, filled with garbage. And I'm not just talking Styrofoam hamburger holders and discarded needles and deadly chemicals that just happen to fall into the river; I'm talking human scum, too. Grifters and drunks and addicts, hookers and dealers and petty thieves. Guys who will mug you if you step into the wrong street and shoot you if you try to call for help. And sometimes, things are so busy and crowded and noisy that you can't tell the scum from the rest of your neighbors.

Gotham City isn't safe anymore. Why can't somebody clean it up? If only it could be like it was yesterday, when everybody had bright, smiling faces, and believed in the American Dream and the value of a dollar. Back in the fifties, when people knew their place and kept their problems to themselves.

Let's go back to those days: the early fifties, a happier time. Let's go back to the happiest time of all, Christmastime.

Our story opens a few months earlier, in a big house on a big street, owned by big people who must have big money. And they have more than that to be happy about today, for this man and woman are having a baby.

But there's a problem.

Father paces back and forth on a landing large enough to house three whole families farther downtown. He nervously puffs on a cigarette. In the other room, we hear the mother's labor pains. The baby's almost here.

Then the moans stop. There is nothing but silence. A moment passes, and a new voice cries out. But there's something about that voice, something about those goos and gahgahs that isn't right.

The door opens. A nurse staggers out, her face blank, as if what she has just seen was so horrendous that her emotions cannot yet comprehend it. Somehow, she manages to put one foot in front of the other and wanders down the hall. Next comes the doctor, and his face is bone white, as if this man who has witnessed death a hundred times has finally seen something worse.

Father can bear it no longer. He rushes by the ashen doctor into the room that holds his wife and child.

There is another moment of silence. But after that, the house is filled with father's screams.

* * *

But I promised you Christmas, and Christmas it will be. So we skip forward a few months. The house is all done up for the holidays, no expense spared, with lights and tinsel and a fine, big, decorated tree. The radio is on, brightly playing the music of the season, as father and mother share a little seasonal cheer.

And baby is there, too, in that playpen. Well, maybe it looks less like a playpen and more like a cage, but baby mustn't get into mischief. Baby looks out at the bright lights as the radio plays.

"He knows when you are sleeping—"

What is that in front of the cage? That nasty family cat is slinking by, but not fast enough for baby.

"He knows when you're awake—"

One good grab, and the cat is gone. A single feline scream, and the cat will never bother baby again.

"He knows when you've been bad or good—"

Baby chirps with happiness. Mother and father are careful to quickly finish their Christmas cheer, and maybe even have a little more.

But you can't have baby cooped up forever.

So later that very same night mother and father decide to take baby for a walk. It's a beautiful winter night, a few snowflakes, perhaps, but nothing to worry about. If you listen, you can hear Christmas carolers. Another pair of happy parents wheel a carriage filled with their tiny bundle of joy through the park, and call out to mother and father.

"Merry Christmas!"

Somehow, father and mother manage to smile as they

pass, but the smiles leave their faces as soon as others can no longer see them. They wheel their carriage with a grim purpose. But look at their carriage, would you? It's a large wicker monstrosity, with leather straps to keep baby exactly in place. Most of all, it looks like something to keep prying eyes away and those weird noises muffled inside.

On go father and mother, on to that storybook bridge overlooking the babbling stream. Father and mother look to the left and look to the right, but it's late, and they are all alone. Without another word, they pick up the carriage together and toss it from the bridge into the roaring stream.

The carriage falls through the freezing air to land in the rapidly running water, where it is carried away, through the open park and trees and hedges of the suburbs, down into the bricks and cement and walls of the city, down to where the stream meets the sewers and goes beneath the great metropolis, where the sweet water joins the murk of Gotham, and the stars no longer shine.

So the carriage travels on through darkness, surrounded by the foulest of stenches and the cries of those things that live without light. But every trip must have a destination. So it is that the carriage goes from one pipe to another to another, until at last the stream around it disgorges the great wheeled cage before a great island of ice.

The carriage washes up on that icy shore, and the baby hears a noise, and realizes he isn't alone. For out of the darkness stride four of the most regal birds you have ever seen, four emperor penguins, to stand guard around their newfound treasure.

* * *

A most warming story, don't you think? But it happened very long ago. Now the baby is all grown up.

Gotham City isn't safe anymore. Pain and death wait for far too many on the city streets.

Trust me. I'm the kind of bird that can make it happen.

CHAPTER
One

Christmastime again. It happens every year.

But today things are different. Today there's Batman. There's a proud father now, showing a sled with that bat on it to his wife. Oops! Have to hide that present, 'cause here comes junior!

And farther out in Gotham City Plaza, there's an adorable little girl who pulls open her precious little purse and pulls out a dollar (a whole dollar!) to give to the Santa Claus collecting for the Salvation Army. It's all pretty sweet, isn't it? People are shopping and caroling and smiling and even skating down at the ice rink set up for the season.

And look! Right here in front of us a young man gives a young woman a poinsettia. And what a kiss she gives him back! Christmas cheer is everywhere, isn't it? Pretty goddamned sweet.

Don't worry. Sweetness can't last forever. Things will get much better very soon.

Uh-oh. Here's that snow bunny, that very well-endowed young lady dressed sort of like an elf, except she has a tiara and a banner that reads "ICE PRINCESS." What a babe. She smiles a truly dazzling smile as she talks into her microphone.

"Could I have your attention, Gotham City?"

And of course Gotham City—all those shoppers and carolers and smilers and kissers—give her their undivided attention. She smiles again, or maybe she never ever stops smiling, and looks over to that elegant lamppost clock, a wonderful re-creation of the real thing, and sees the big hand reach a quarter to seven.

Once again, her excited voice chirps over the microphone: "It's time for tonight's lighting of the tree! How about that?"

She presses a big, multicolored button before her. And what happens next? Why, the whole big Gotham Plaza Christmas tree lights up, of course! No surprises.

At least not yet.

"Aah!" the crowd proclaims as they watch the tree. "Oooh!"

But a surprise is coming soon.

Wait a moment, you ask. Who's telling us all this? Who is this in the dark? When he looks through that sewer grate, does it remind him of some time long ago, when he looked out of the bars of his playpen at the bright Christmas lights, when he looked out of his wicker carriage at the river that surrounded him?

But baby is baby no more. He's grown bigger now, much bigger, and he's learned a thing or two. For one thing, he's learned a jaunty little tune. If you'll permit me, I'll sing:

"I know when you've been sleeping, I know when you're awake—"

Soon.

CHAPTER
Two

A butler's work was never done.

Alfred dodged and wove his way through the Christmas shoppers with the ease of a seasoned veteran. He had performed these sorts of errands for more than forty years, first for Thomas Wayne and his wife, and then, after that couple's tragic death, for their growing son Bruce. On these last days before the holiday he would fetch the Christmas goose, a few new ornaments for the tree, and perhaps some small presents for friends and acquaintances of his employer.

At least, he thought, in doing this he could make life a little easier for Master Bruce. In these last few months, Bruce Wayne had had certain other things on his mind.

"Paper!" the newsboy shouted as Alfred approached.

"Read about the latest sighting of the Penguin creature! Read all about it! Missing link between man and bird? Get your paper!"

Alfred studied the lurid headline on the *Gotham Herald* with a single practiced glance:

PENGUIN:
MAN OR MYTH
OR SOMETHING WORSE?

The newsboy held a paper out in front of the butler. "Paper, mister?"

"Dear boy," Alfred replied. "Sometimes it is a diversion to read such piffle." He frowned down at the headline. "Most times it is a *waste* of time."

Alfred continued to frown as the newsboy turned away. He could have sworn he saw something moving down in that sewer grate. No doubt it was nothing more than the reflection of the Christmas lights.

It was almost as if he expected something to be lurking in the shadows. Alfred chuckled. If he didn't watch himself, he'd get as bad as Master Bruce.

Who did the Mayor think Max was, some kind of ordinary citizen?

Max Shreck told himself to calm down. The Mayor had arrived here in the Shreck corporate offices, after all, even if it had been hours after he had been summoned. And, Max reminded himself, he had to be pleasant to this windbag politician, at least until the Mayor gave him what he wanted.

The Mayor nodded out at the view of the Christmas tree, all lit up down in Gotham Plaza. "Well, here's hoping"— he beat his fist upon the desk—"knock wood—Gotham might just have its first merry Christmas in a good long while."

So His Honor was growing sentimental? Max figured it was time to turn on the charm. "I feel almost vulgar," he said with a nod and a smile, "in this Yuletide context, about mentioning the new power plant." He paused to pound his own fist into his open palm. "But if we're going to break ground when we've got to break ground, I need permits, variances, tax incentives"—he paused again to shrug apologetically—"that kind of pesky nonsense."

The Mayor looked at Max as if he had never heard of this power plant. Which, of course, he hadn't. But Max Shreck never let a detail like that get in his way.

"Power plant?" the Mayor objected. "Max, our studies show that Gotham has enough energy to sustain growth into the next centu—"

Shreck cut him off with a hearty laugh. "Your analysts are talking growth at one percent per annum. That's not growth, that's a mild swelling. I'm planning ahead for a revitalized Gotham City!" He waved at all the pretty lights on the far side of the plate-glass window. "So we can light the whole plaza without worrying about brownouts." He turned and frowned critically at the Mayor. "Do you like the sound of *brownouts*? Do you?"

He glanced away from the politician for the merest of instants as the door to his office opened, admitting his son Chip and his secretary, Selina Kyle. It must be almost time. He would have to wrap this up.

He opened all ten of his fingers before the Mayor's face. "Imagine a Gotham City of the future lit up like a blanket of stars." He closed his fists, then opened and closed them again. "But blinking, on and off?" He shook his head. "Embarrassingly low on juice? Frankly, I cringe, Mr. Mayor."

Chip moved quickly but quietly across the room toward his father. With the respect he showed for his old man, you'd hardly suspect that this boy was a star college quarterback. But Max liked it that way, both the college star and the respect. In fact, he demanded it be that way.

"Dad," Chip interrupted as he glanced at the large digital clock on the wall. "Mr. Mayor. It's time to go downstairs and bring joy to the masses."

Uh-oh, Shreck thought. His pitch to the Mayor was really running a little bit behind schedule. But Max wouldn't let His Honor off that easily. He fixed the Mayor with his best Shreck smile.

"Sorry," the Mayor replied dismissively before Max could add another word. "You'll have to submit reports, blueprints, and plans through the usual committees, through the usual channels."

Max almost lost his smile. Who did this two-bit politician think he was talking to? But he couldn't let the Mayor go now, not when he was so close. There had to be some way to make Jenkins see the error of his ways.

Selina put down a tray bearing a silver coffeepot and a couple of fine china cups. "Um," she mentioned somewhat hesitantly, "I had a suggestion. Well, actually, more of just a question—"

Max's gaze locked upon her, silencing her instantly. He

had to be nice to the Mayor; being nice to Selina was something else altogether. What did she think she was doing, butting in? Didn't she know a secretary's place?

"I'm afraid we haven't properly housebroken Ms. Kyle," he apologized to the Mayor. He smiled as he waved at the tray. "In the plus column, though, she brews one hell of a cup of coffee!"

But he had to get away from these sorts of interruptions if he was going to get Jenkins in his corner. Max pushed the Mayor from the office without touching the pot or the cups.

Selina looked after her disappearing boss. What had she done?

Corn dog!

Chip smiled at her, the kind of smile that probably melted college coeds at his feet. It was too bad the smile was as phony as Chip's part-time job for his father.

"Thanks," he said, waving gallantly at the coffee tray. "Anyway, it's not the caffeine that gets us buzzed around here. It's the obedience."

He favored her with one more of his winning smiles before he turned and strode out after his father.

She waited until he was out of the room before she replied.

"Shut up, Chip."

Selina stared at the tray before her for a second, then slapped her forehead with her palm. " *Actually more of a question.*' You stupid corn dog!"

She wanted to get ahead, show Mr. Shreck that she was really worthy of the title of administrative assistant. But all she ever did was open her mouth enough so that her foot could fit right in. She had seen the look her boss had given her. After an outburst like hers, she was lucky to still have a job.

"Corn dog." She slapped herself again for good measure. *"Corn dog!"*

Couldn't she ever do anything right?

As soon as Chip had caught up with them, Max took the Mayor down the executive elevator, then guided him right through the first floor of Shreck's Department Store, so important to Gotham's economy. When Shreck's prospered, the city prospered, too. The Mayor knew that already, but Max figured it wouldn't hurt to remind him. They just happened to go out of the main door, too, right by the large SHRECK'S sign, featuring that happy Shreck cat that all of Gotham loved. *All of Gotham!* But the Mayor should know that, too. It was a symbol of everything Max stood for, and, maybe, a sign of even greater things to come.

The minute they stepped from the store, the news media gathered around. Flashbulbs popped in their faces, questions were shouted in their ears, TV cameras swiveled to follow their every move; all the price of fame. Max nodded pleasantly, the Mayor waved, Chip smiled, as all of Gotham gathered around.

Their entourage walked across the plaza as Max spotted the Salvation Army Santa. What a photo opportunity! It was time for some positive image making. Max paused and reached for his wallet. He passed two bills to Santa, and the one on top was a fifty. The flashbulbs popped merrily.

The Salvation Army guy frowned as he saw that the second bill was a single. Pretty smart Santa. It didn't matter, though, because the cameras had moved on to follow Max, Chip, and the Mayor. The Salvation Army Santa was already old news.

His son tugged at his sleeve. "Watch your step, Dad. It's pretty grotesque."

Max looked ahead to the river of melting sludge that his son pointed to. Chip was right. There was some incredible filth in this town. Max redirected his steps to the dry patch on the far side of the sewer grate.

Max frowned. When his eyes had followed the path of the sludge into the sewer, he almost thought he saw something down below. Not a rat, that's the sort of thing he'd expect. It was much bigger than a rat. No, it looked more like somebody holding an umbrella.

An umbrella?

Max shrugged off the thought. He was on top of the world. What did it matter to him what—or who—lived in the sewer these days?

CHAPTER
Three

C orn dog.
    Selina looked at the Post-It notes tacked onto her computer, reminders that would help her fit in, help her to get ahead in the competitive world of Shreck Industries.

"Don't 'get' jokes," said one. Max didn't like it when she got too clever.

"Save it for your diary," read another. The upper echelon here at Shreck didn't want to hear about her problems. In fact, they didn't want to hear about anything except making money.

But none of the half-dozen notes in front of her got down to the basics of why she kept screwing up around here. If she could just get a grip on where she was falling short, if she could simply come up with that one golden rule she should remember so that Max and all his cronies would smile on her next time promotions came around.

But what did Max really want?

As soon as she asked herself the question, Selina knew the answer. It was so simple, a single word.

"Obey."

Selina wrote it on a Post-It note and stuck it on top of the others.

Beyond her window, she could hear the cheering crowd, waiting for Max to give his speech. The phone rang. She let it. It was such a bad day she didn't want to talk to anybody else.

She shouldn't be here, anyway, she should be down below, shouldn't she? But doing what? She frowned, sure she was forgetting something. Her eyes wandered over to the legal pad by the still-ringing phone.

There, on the bright yellow pad, in big block letters, was the word "SPEECH." Max's speech. The speech she had written, and then neglected to give to Max.

Oh, no. She was in for it this time.

"Darn." She hit herself on the forehead all over again. Who was the biggest corn dog of all?

Max couldn't let it go. He was not the sort of man to wait. He had to have the Mayor's okay, and he wanted it now. If the Mayor wouldn't give it to him the easy way, he'd just have to take it any way he could.

"I have enough signatures," he said, still smiling, "from Shreck employees alone, to warrant a recall of a Mayor who isn't doing his job." He graciously motioned for the Mayor to precede him onto the dais. "That's not a threat," he added. "Just simple math."

But the Mayor smiled back at him as he walked ahead. "Maybe," he replied. "But you don't have an issue, Max. Nor do you have a candidate."

Max followed His Honor up onto the platform. Both received an obligatory peck upon the cheek from the Ice Princess before they took their places. The clock behind the podium read five minutes to seven. It was time to get this show moving.

Professional that he was, the Mayor grabbed the microphone. "The man who's given this city so much is here, to keep giving," His Honor announced to the masses. "Welcome Gotham's own Santa Claus, Max Shreck!"

Max thought the Mayor was pushing it a little bit. Gotham's own Santa Claus? There was such a thing as being too sincere. Still, there wasn't a crowd in all of Gotham that the head of Shreck Industries couldn't win over.

He opened his executive portfolio. There was nothing inside.

Chip frowned over his shoulder, that "Is there something wrong, Dad?" look on his face.

"Forgot," he said to Chip between extremely clenched teeth.

"My," he added.

"Speech," he concluded.

"Remind me to take it out on Selina," he amended as an afterthought.

Well, he'd been in worse fixes than this, and he'd get through this one, too. He'd just have to wing it.

His clenched teeth turned into a magnanimous smile as he faced the crowd. "Santa Claus? 'Fraid not. I'm just a poor little schmo who got a little lucky, and sue me if I want to give a little back."

He waved to the pile of brightly wrapped packages between him and his son; the same sort of worthless trinkets the store gave out every year. He wasn't even too sure what was in the boxes this year, except that it came from whatever items his store had overstocked.

"I only wish I could hand out more than just expensive baubles," he continued effusively. "In this season of our Savior's birth, I wish I could hand out World Peace, and Unconditional Love, wrapped in a big bow."

Max wanted to give everyone a present, wrapped in a big bow?

"Oh, but you can," murmured the squat man beneath the umbrella. "Oh, but you will." He opened the ornate pocket watch that he held; a little rusted perhaps, but still elegant. And it kept perfect time.

Time? It was one minute till.

Time to close the umbrella.

CHAPTER
Four

Alfred managed to skirt the last few happy shoppers as Max Shreck launched into his speech. The man was speaking absolute drivel, and the crowd was actually cheering him on. Oh, well, the butler thought, it probably had something to do with the spirit of Christmas. He supposed he could be a little more charitable as well. Still, he was happy to be leaving this madhouse before it became any worse.

He stopped to put the packages down so that he might unlock the door of the Rolls. It was at that moment that he realized there was a parking ticket on his windshield. A parking ticket? What did that have to do with the spirit of Christmas? Certainly, the members of the constabulary were only doing their job, but still, wouldn't their effort be better served if they were out tracking down the criminals rampant in this town rather than indulging in parking tickets?

The crowd's roar grew twice as loud as before. Despite his better judgment, Alfred took one final look back at the throng. There, above their heads, he could see some sort of gigantic box, wrapped up in bright paper and colorful ribbons, like some monstrous Christmas present. And the cheers at this monstrosity's arrival were deafening.

The big clock in the middle of the mall struck seven. In fact, all the clocks in every store up and down the street struck seven, increasing the din even more.

Alfred plucked the ticket from the windshield and walked over to the driver's side of the car. He wouldn't be getting out of here a moment too soon.

Max's mind went blank when he saw the box. It looked like a present the size of a house. And not a small house, either.

"Great idea," the mayor remarked. For the first time tonight, Max could hear genuine admiration in the politician's voice.

"But not mine," Max had to admit. He had to get on with his speech. Or did he? The way the crowd was cheering now, he doubted if they could hear anything else he would say. He looked forward to the edge of the stage, where his son had moved to hand out the presents to the crowd, but the first of the gifts had fallen from Chip's hands to land on top of the sewer grate before the podium. Chip stood, frozen, watching the giant present make its way through the square toward them.

* * *

What was this? A small, wrapped gift had fallen upon the grating, right up above his vantage point?

The squat man chuckled. "Deck the halls," he whispered.

How generous of them. And how appropriate, for he was about to give all of Gotham City a present of his very own.

CHAPTER
Five

I t was all part of the job, Commissioner Gordon thought, but he didn't have to be happy with it. Especially when the crowd grew as large as it did for the Shreck's annual Christmas giveaway.

There was always the potential for disaster when there were this many people in this confined a space. And then Shreck insisted on letting his son toss out freebies to the crowd! But was even that bad enough? No, now that publicity-mad store owner had to come up with this giant gift gimmick, without even informing the police about it beforehand!

There must, Gordon thought, be some statute they could haul Shreck in on, if only to make him see reason next time. But the mayor would never allow it. Shreck was a big campaign contributor, after all. Not to mention a great source of photo opportunities.

Oh, well, Gordon had to look on the bright side. This would all be over in the next few minutes. No one had been killed yet. And at least he got to sit in his police cruiser, outside of the crush of the crowd, and away from the long-winded speechmaking of Max Shreck.

Gordon turned his attention back to this huge box that was rolling into the square. It was designed like one of those floats in the Christmas parade. Looking at the bottom of the box, he could make out wheels at each of the corners propelling the float along; not truck wheels, though, they were too thin and closely spaced for that. Gordon would guess that the float was being moved by four motorcycles. And in between the cycles, the commissioner could see walking feet. He wondered if there was going to be a second part to this presentation.

Gordon shook his head. This seemed like an awful lot of trouble, even for a media shark like Shreck. He decided he'd better call the other units stationed around the plaza. Who knew what problems they'd have with crowd control if this gift opened up?

Corn dog!

She would never get anywhere if she just sat around and moped! If Max hadn't taken his speech, it was her job to bring it down to him! Selina grabbed the envelope that contained her carefully worded season's greetings, and headed for the elevator.

She just hoped she wasn't too late.

* * *

Gordon stopped talking into the police radio.

Gotham Plaza had gone crazy.

The giant package burst open. Three men on motorcycles roared out, right into the crowd. People tried to run, screaming, frantic to get away from the growling engines.

A fourth cycle ripped out of the side of the box, jumped the railing above the plaza and landed in the middle of the crowd gathered for the tree lighting.

Some of the people didn't make it, and were flattened or tossed aside by the marauding cycles. A fifth cyclist emerged from hiding to follow the first three. The crowd was too tightly packed. They had nowhere to escape.

And the box still had more surprises.

The top opened. Five acrobats sprang out, cartwheeling into the panicked crowd to knock down anyone still left standing. One of them kayoed a mounted patrolman. Another flipped beyond the nearby onlookers, straight toward a mobile soup-kitchen Shreck had set up for the homeless. The kitchen volunteers barely escaped as the acrobats' fists and feet smashed everything in sight.

The other acrobats had another goal. They were headed straight for the platform with the Christmas tree!

Confusion was everywhere. Calls came in to Gordon from the other cars, asking for directions. The panicked crowd surged away from the plaza to surround the commisoner's car. People were climbing over each other in their rush to escape. Someone was going to get crushed out there. A sled crashed into the windshield of Gordon's cruiser.

Something had to be done now. And there was only one person who could do it.

The police commissioner found his voice again. "What are you waiting for?" he barked into his radio. "The signal!"

CHAPTER
Six

Bruce Wayne sat in the darkness. Alfred hadn't returned home from his Christmas errands yet, and Bruce was all alone in Wayne Manor. Alone in the dark and quiet; alone with his thoughts.

Bruce didn't like going out in crowds much at night. It reminded him too much of another winter night, when he was only a boy. His parents had taken him into downtown Gotham City earlier on that day, and they had all stayed until long after dark. They had had a wonderful time that day, going shopping, having dinner, going to a show. Bruce could never remember having such a good time with his parents. It was a day filled with nothing but laughter.

And then—

Bruce closed his eyes, but he could still see the gunman who stepped out of the shadows to rob his parents. He could still see his father put up a fight, see his mother's mouth open as she cried for help. And he saw the double flash of the gun as two bullets killed both father and mother.

They had taken his parents away from him.

Now he would make them pay.

He opened his eyes and saw the light shining in the window; the symbol, a silhouette of a bat in a pool of yellow light.

Bruce smiled.

He was needed.

This was going so well. First the cyclists, then the acrobats, and now the rest of his merry band. It was getting to be a real circus.

The Fire Breather smashed the window of the toy store. He stuck that rod of his in his mouth, and breathed fire over the whole display window. The entire place went up in flames. That precious Ice Princess ran away, pushing an elderly woman to the ground. Oh, dear, look at the old bag. She'd fallen and she couldn't get up. In a minute or two, she was sure to be trampled.

The squat creature laughed from his vantage point beneath the sewer grate. If all went according to plan, this was the last night he would ever have to watch the world from down here. Soon, he would be up there again with all the fat cats, and all those "haves" would look up to him, because he'd have more than all of them combined.

He saw a beacon split the sky. He'd know that black and yellow signal anywhere, and it only made him laugh that much harder.

"Ooh, Batman," he said in his odd, raspy voice. "I'm tremblin'."

CHAPTER
Seven

The elevator had taken forever to get to the top floor. Selina had jumped in it as soon as it had opened, pounding the down button and hoping that she was still in time to salvage some portion of her boss's speech. Thankfully, nobody else was going down just then, and she made the descent in under a minute. She ran through the lobby and out the main door of the department store.

Boy, it sure was noisy out here. For a second, she was almost happy her boss never let her attend these things. Now where was he in all these people?

Three motorcycles burst out of the crowd, headed straight for her. She jumped back out of the way as the cycles roared on by, still almost brushing her clothes.

If she hadn't jumped she would have been crushed. Boy,

35

she thought, all those workouts at the gym had actually done her some good.

But why weren't those cyclists looking where they were going? They could really hurt somebody! And the way everybody was screaming; was something wrong down here?

This was crazy.

An organ grinder, with a big red organ box and handlebar mustaches, was the first one on the stage. And he had the usual monkey—except that this monkey had a gun.

Max hoped it was a cap gun.

The Organ Grinder grinned and turned his box toward the Christmas tree. He twisted the handle. Bullets spewed out of the box. It was a Gatling gun! Ornaments and lights exploded under the hail of bullets.

"Take, that, tannenbaum!" the grinder yelled.

But there were other newcomers on the stage now—a grossly fat clown, another guy, dressed in rags, who kept sticking a sword down his throat, and this very colorfully dressed woman. For once in Max's life, he wasn't all that interested in the curves beneath that woman's costume, probably because a large portion of her costume consisted of rows and rows of knives.

Both the Mayor and Chip moved toward the back of the platform. Max wanted to join them. But where could they run?

"Relax," the lady with the knives remarked. "We just came for the guy who runs the show."

The Mayor stepped forward. Max was impressed. He never thought the weasel had that kind of guts.

"What do you want from me?" the mayor asked.

The Sword Swallower laughed and pushed His Honor off the stage.

"Not you," the fellow somehow said around his sword. "Shreck."

Him? Max thought. Where could he run? Where could he hide? But good old Chip stepped in the way. That gave Max a moment more to plan his escape.

"All this courage," the clown remarked drolly. "Goose-bump city."

And with that, the Knife Lady whipped one of her blades straight at Chip, nicking his ear. Oh, God, Max thought, they were both in danger.

"Son!" Max called out

"Dad!" Chip called back. "Save yourself!"

But Max had already leapt from the platform and was heading for the crowd at a dead run.

Chip looked across the plaza and realized this mad scene was going to get wilder still.

There, on the far side of the crowd, he saw the Bat-mobile.

CHAPTER
Eight

Alfred was trapped by the surging crowd, still mere feet from the safety of the Rolls. At the very minute that he had been about to reenter his car, that large box had burst open, sending the crowd into a panic and pushing him a dozen feet away from his goal.

There the car sat, bulletproof, shatterproof, with a phone inside with which he might be able to call Master Bruce and summon help, and there was no way he could reach it. Everyone was screaming and pushing futilely one against the other, but the crowd seemed trapped by its very density, without direction.

And the criminals only wanted to make it worse. A thug on a motorcycle plowed through the masses only a few feet in front of him while three stilt-walkers started kicking the crowd from behind. With all these miscreants in costume, Alfred thought, it was like some nightmare version of the circus.

He heard the roar of engines, not motorcycles this time, but a deeper sound, and one that he believed he recognized.

Alfred looked back to the plaza and smiled at last.

The Batmobile had arrived.

Blades shot from either side of the Batmobile, smashing through two different stilts in an instant. A pair of stilt-walkers fell to the ground face first.

But they were not out of danger yet. Alfred saw a circus strongman, all rippling muscles beneath his tight-fitting costume, bearing down upon them. It looked as if the butler would have to rescue the little girl.

The Strongman was gaining on them. Alfred glanced over to see that the Batmobile was shooting some of its arsenal, small black Batdiscs that whirled straight for the gangsters terrorizing the crowd. The Batmobile turned in Alfred's direction.

Now.

Alfred ducked as another Batdisc sailed over his head to connect with the Strongman's cranium. The Tattooed Strongman fell, quite unconscious. Alfred stood again and smiled as the Batmobile wheeled past.

That was very nicely done.

Max couldn't believe it. He had gotten away. It just proved, he guessed, what a pair of still-speedy legs and a bellyful of fear can do for you. But that fear could only take him so far. He had to stop for a moment, to catch his breath and decide on his next move. He darted down a side street, free at last of all but a few members of the screaming mob.

Max's steps slowed even more as he felt hot air coming up from a sewer grate below his feet. It felt oddly warm and reassuring compared to the winter chill around him, especially now that the sweat on his face and hands was exposed to the Gotham wind.

Maybe he should stop here for a moment or two and reconnoiter, perhaps figure out exactly what was going on here. After all, he had just survived threats from criminals, a speedy chase, and a near capture.

For the first time, Max wondered if there was some way he could turn all this to his advantage.

Action always helped.

He'd taken care of the worst of this band of thugs in the middle of Gotham Plaza. Now he had to mop up the trash on the outskirts. He turned the Batmobile toward three more of the criminals who seemed intent on destroying the surrounding stores.

These three were dressed as clowns. Batman found that particularly appropriate. He angled the Batmobile slightly so that all three were directly in his path, then pressed the accelerator. The clowns turned and fired on him. The bullets bounced harmlessly off the car's exoskeleton as the Batmobile sped toward its prey.

One clown managed to jump free, but the other two bounced smartly off the hood. He'd come back for the third in a moment. Batman turned the wheel to follow another fellow who was breathing fire on the window displays of a toy store.

Wait a moment. Both of those clowns had still managed to cling to the hood, and one was firing at his windshield. And that clown he missed was firing at him from behind. Sometimes, these felons simply didn't know when they were beaten.

Batman hit the brakes.

The Batmobile stopped abruptly, launching both clowns forward into the Fire Breather. All three of them fell into the smashed window display.

Batman had one clown to go.

He twisted the knob to activate the hydraulic lift. In a matter of seconds, the lift's steel framework unfolded from the car's undercarriage and jacked the entire Batmobile off the ground, spinning the vehicle completely around so that the toy store was now to the Batmobile's rear.

Batman heard a noise behind him as he gunned the engine again. Somehow, the Fire Breather had regained his feet. He jumped from the window, ready to breathe his flame on the Batmobile.

Batman floored the accelerator. The Fire Breather was caught in the exhaust. Batman checked the scene in his rearview mirror. This time, the Fire Breather went up in flame. All lit up, Batman thought, like a Christmas tree.

Now what was that last clown up to?

Maybe Batman could give him a hot time, too.

CHAPTER
Nine

Selina supposed it was too late to give Max his speech. In fact, the way this crowd was moving, it seemed to be too late to do much of anything.

Then she had this clown grab her. A guy actually dressed in a clown suit pulled her from the steps and stuck the muzzle of a gun against her neck.

He muttered something about "Never taking me alive."

Somehow, Selina doubted he wanted to start a conversation. She heard something crack as the clown dragged her in front of him. Somehow, she managed to look down and saw that her brand-new heel had snapped off her brand-new fashion pump.

That was it, Selina thought. Those heels cost her money.

Now she was mad.

"I probably shouldn't bring this up," she said pointedly to the terrifying Clown, "but this is a very serious pair of shoes you ruined."

The terrifying Clown stared at her in astonishment.

"Couldn't you have just been a prince," she continued, "and broken my jaw? My body will heal, but that was the last pair left in my size!"

"All these innocent bystanders and I *had* to pick you?" the terrifying Clown asked.

Selina opened her mouth to respond.

"Shut up!" the Clown hissed.

Boy, Selina thought, somebody around here had really gotten up on the wrong side of the bed. This creep had his gun stuck in her face now. Maybe, she considered, she should be worried about more than her shoe.

The Batmobile screeched to a halt in front of them. The door flew open and a man dressed all in black leapt out and headed straight for them. It was Batman.

An acrobat somersaulted out of the crowd. These circus people were everywhere. He headed straight for the man in black, whose muscular costume also featured a very good-looking cowl and cape.

Batman punched the acrobat's lights out with one very well-placed fist.

This got the terrifying Clown's attention. He waved his gun at the Batman for an instant, then quickly brought the muzzle back to Selina.

"Listen up, Mister Man-bat," he said very loudly in Selina's ear. "You take one step closer and I'll—"

Batman looked back and smiled.

"Sure" was all he said.

He whipped out some sort of gun from a holster on his hip and fired a spear toward the clown. The clown jerked his head away as the spear buried itself into the wall behind them.

The terrifying Clown started to laugh. "Oh, *nice* shot, mister—"

But Batman wasn't through. There was a line connected to the spear, a line Batman tugged sharply. A piece of wall fell forward with the spear, right on the head of the terrifying Clown. The gunman staggered. Selina saw her chance.

"You shouldn't have left the other heel." She drove the point of her remaining shoe into the terrifying Clown's knee, making him lose his balance the rest of the way. Clown and gun went tumbling to the ground.

Batman stepped forward and leaned over his fallen foe. A gloved hand reached down and brushed at a crimson triangle tattoo over the terrifying Clown's left eye. Selina stared. Was that significant?

The Batman, hero to millions, and pretty well built besides, was mere inches away from her. Come on, Selina thought. This is the chance of a lifetime. Say something!

"Wow," she began. "The Batman—or is it just 'Batman'?"

He didn't reply. She tried to smile.

"Your choice," she added. "Of course."

Batman looked up, and for a moment their eyes met. He

had very nice eyes. She thought she saw the slightest bit of a smile beneath his mask.

"Gotta go," he said.

And he was gone, half a block away in a matter of seconds, off to talk with Commissioner Gordon. The crowd gathered around the two and started to cheer.

That was it? Her big meeting with Batman? Not that she could blame him. It was no wonder he didn't wait around, with her terrible attempts at conversation.

"Well, that was—very brief," she murmured. "Like most men in my life." She chuckled caustically. "*What* men?"

She looked down at the unconscious clown at her feet. "Well, there's you but, let's face it, you need therapy."

She knelt beside the clown and picked up his gun. She had never gotten a close look at the weapon when it was pressed into her neck. It wasn't a regular gun at all. It had more of a futuristic look to it, like it shot out electricity or something.

She pointed it at the clown. Whoops, maybe she pulled the trigger. The clown stiffened for a second, as if he'd been hit by a jolt from the gun. So she'd definitely pulled the trigger.

"Electroshock therapy," she reassured the still-unconscious body. "What a bargain. Now we both feel better."

Max heard the sound of cheers. Maybe all the carnage was over. Maybe he should go back and join the celebration.

The sewer grate he was standing on opened up.

Max fell before he could even utter a proper scream. And as he fell, he saw the sewer grate pop back into place overhead.

He landed in something soft. But he didn't stop moving.

Something had grabbed him around the ankles. And that something was dragging him into the darkness.

For the sake of form, Max screamed for real.

CHAPTER
Ten

T hanks for saving the day, Batman," Commissioner
Gordon said in all sincerity. "Thanks for making the
rest of us look like a bunch of dolts." He laughed, a trace
of envy in his voice, but he shook his head as he watched
his men rounding up the wounded thugs. "I'm afraid the
Red Triangle Circus Gang is back."

Batman surveyed the remains of the carnage around him.
"We'll see" was his only reply.

Gordon wanted to ask exactly what Batman meant by
that. But the Mayor showed up before the commissioner
could say another word.

"The Caped Crusader!" the Mayor bubbled. "We don't
deserve you!" He smiled as a news photographer snapped

a picture. "They almost made off with our mover and shaker, Max Shreck. But—"

His Honor stopped and frowned, looking back to the speaker's platform and the decimated Christmas tree. In a lower voice, he added, "Where is that insufferable son of a bitch?"

He looked back to Batman. But Batman was no longer there. Gordon couldn't help but smile at His Honor's consternation. Batman had no need to stand around and listen to self-important politicians.

Gordon envied Batman more than ever.

Selina threw open the door to her apartment.

"Honey, I'm home!"

She waited for the answering silence before finishing the joke.

"Oh, I forgot. I'm not married."

It was an old joke, but it was her joke. She laughed dutifully as she looked around her studio digs: the pink wall-to-wall carpet that went so well with her off-white furniture, her fully stocked dollhouse, that quilt she'd get around to finishing someday, her substantial collection of stuffed animals, and that neon "HELLO THERE" sign that would greet her when there was no man to do the job. Plus, of course, she had a Christmas tree to cheer the place up even more. Now, if her job would only allow her enough time to enjoy this place. Oh, well. A working woman couldn't have everything.

She opened up the closet and hung up her long winter coat, realizing, as it bumped heavily against the wall, that the pocket still contained the stun gun she had taken from the clown. Oh, well, she thought again. She pulled the gun from the pocket and looked down at it. A woman also couldn't have too much protection.

An accusatory meow caused her to turn to the half-open window. There was her cat, returned from her nightly prowling in time to eat.

"Miss Kitty!" Selina greeted her as she walked over to the kitchen counter. "Back from more sexual escapades you refuse to share." She put the gun down and pulled a bowl from the cupboard, then opened the refrigerator door. "Not that I'd ever pry."

She frowned. She was out of cat food again. Ah, there was the milk. She poured some in the bowl and set it on the floor. "Drink your dinner."

Miss Kitty walked regally from the window, as if by simply having the good grace to return to the apartment, the milk was no less than her just reward. Selina collapsed back against the counter, totally exhausted. Sometimes she wished she could have the carefree life of a cat.

She looked down at Miss Kitty, contentedly lapping at the milk. "What did you just purr?" She changed her voice, trying to make it sound more catlike. " 'How can anyone be so pathetic?' "

Selina nodded in resignation as she resumed her normal tone. "Yes, to you I seem pathetic. But I'm a working girl. I've got to pay the rent. Maybe if you were chipping in, instead of stepping out—"

She let the rest of the sentence hang in the air, and walked over to the phone machine, perched in the midst of pictures of Selina in happier, less hurried times: on a trampoline as a kid; her fifteenth birthday with her horse;

that time she climbed the mountain during a college vacation. She used to have time to really get exercise. Now she was lucky if she could run for the subway.

She pressed the play button on her answering machine, then turned and pulled down the old-fashioned Murphy bed from its niche in the wall.

"Selina, dear," the first message began. It was her mother's voice, in her stern this-is-going-to-be-for-your-own-good voice. "It's your mother, just calling to say hello—"

"Yeah, right," Selina murmured, anticipating what came next, "but—"

"—but," her mother continued right on cue, "I'm disappointed that you're not coming home for Christmas. I wanted to discuss just why you insist on languishing in Gotham City as some lowly secretary when you—"

"Lowly *assistant*," Selina corrected as she reached back to punch the fast forward button. "Thank you."

She released the button as she heard the beep that signaled the beginning of the next message.

"Selina, about that Christmas getaway we planned?" It was her boyfriend Paul, sounding even wimpier than usual. "I'll be going alone." He paused as if afraid to continue, then added in a rush, "Dr. Shaw says I need to be my own person now, and not an appendage—"

"Some appendage," Selina remarked ruefully as she fast forwarded again. "The party never stops on Selina Kyle's phone answering machine." She sighed. "I guess I should have let him win that last racquetball game."

Another beep, another message.

"Selina," the gruff woman's voice began. "We've

missed you at the rape prevention class.'' Her lecturing tone was almost as good as Selina's mother's. ''It is not enough to master martial arts. Hey, Elvis knew those moves, and he died fat. You must stop seeing yourself as a victi—''

She fast forwarded one more time.

''Hi, Selina.'' An all-too-familiar voice this time. ''This is yourself calling. To remind you, honey, that you have to come back to the office unless you remembered to bring home the Bruce Wayne file, because the meeting's on Wednesday and Max Slavemaster wants every pertinent fact at your lovely tapered fingertips!''

Oh, no! How could she have forgotten—well, she knew exactly how, what with the clown and all. But still! Selina lifted the stun gun from the counter and fired it at the answering machine, jolting it to silence.

''The file!'' she murmured. ''You stupid corn dog! Corn dog! Deep-fried corn dog!''

She went back to the closet to fetch her coat. So much for a good night's sleep.

She was slowly going crazy. Why not make it simple, she thought, and do it all at once?

For some reason, Miss Kitty meowed good-bye.

CHAPTER
Eleven

Max opened his eyes. He was having trouble focusing. He hadn't remembered going to sleep, in fact didn't remember much at all after he had run away from a bunch of crazy circus performers.

He definitely couldn't remember how he'd gotten here, wherever he was.

He turned his head. There, inches away, was a penguin staring back at him.

A penguin?

Max yelped.

The penguin flapped its wings and yelped back.

Max turned back to the chair beneath him and yelled all over again. He was dazed.

And facing him, smiling at him, were all those circus crazies.

There, in front of him, was the Organ Grinder with his monkey, the Tattooed Strongman, that lady with the throwing knives, the guy who swallowed swords, a woman with a boa constrictor looped around her arm and waist, and a ratty-looking lady with a ratty-looking poodle, not to mention all those clowns, acrobats, and stilt-walkers.

They all stared back at Max. What's more, they snickered. But then the snickering stopped, replaced by a respectful silence, as if all the circus people were expecting something.

Max could hear the hum of a huge electrical generator in the background, and saw where it powered a huge air conditioner at the other end of the room. Neither one of them looked very safe; the air conditioner was covered with grime, and he could see sparks flying from the generator even from his vantage point.

And to either side of the generator and air conditioner, there were—penguins.

Even more penguins?

There were hundreds of the critters. Big penguins and small penguins, walking and sitting and flapping and playing across the ice. There were penguins all over this place!

Max heard another sound beyond the generator, a loud dripping sound.

Drip. Drip. Drip.

He turned to his left. There, among the penguins, was a particularly large one, holding an open umbrella. Max watched the drops of water hit the black fabric with a sinister regularity.

Drip. Drip. Drip.

An umbrella?

Drip. Drip. Drip.

The penguin with the umbrella waddled forward, beyond the falling water. And not only was this bird big, but Max could swear it was wearing a union suit.

A union suit?

Yes, it was tattered and filthy, but it was a union suit. And the bird wore a pair of scuffed and well-worn shoes. Maybe, Max thought, he had simply lost his mind. It would be the simplest explanation.

It got worse. The bird closed the umbrella.

It wasn't a penguin.

It was The Penguin.

A small, rotund creature with beady eyes and a beaklike nose stared back at Max. He looked like nothing so much as one of the fowls from which he got his name. The Penguin. The star of the tabloids. The legendary bird-beast from beneath the streets.

The Penguin grinned.

"Hi," he remarked.

Max opened his mouth to scream again, but it was beyond him. No sound came out at all.

"I believe the word you're looking for is"—The Penguin paused to take a breath—"AAAAUUUGGGHHH!"

Max still didn't get anything out. He wasn't sure he'd be able to get anything out ever again.

"Actually," The Penguin reassured him most jovially,

"this is all just a bad dream. You're home in bed. Heavily sedated. Resting comfortably. And dying from the carcinogens you've personally spewed in a lifetime of profiteering. Tragic irony or poetic justice? You tell me."

Max remembered to breathe. That helped.

"My God," he managed. "It's true. The Penguin. Man of the sewers. Please don't hurt—"

"Quiet, Max!" The Penguin snapped. "What do you think, this is a conversation?"

Max quieted. The Penguin twirled his umbrella, pressing something down on the handle. The top of the umbrella spit a great gout of fire. The Penguin nodded happily, quite pleased with the display. He glanced again at Shreck.

"Odd as it may seem, Max, we have something in common. We're both perceived as monsters. But somehow, you're a well-respected monster. And I am"—he looked humbly down at his dirty suit—"to date—*not*."

With that, The Penguin bent down. Max noticed he had a whole pile of umbrellas at his feet. Shreck wondered if all the others were weapons, too. The Penguin picked up a new umbrella. It was the first time the businessman had taken a good look at the birdman's hands. Except that they only sort of looked like hands. They also sort of looked like flippers. The Penguin smiled at Max's attention, and pointed the umbrella as if this one might shoot something else.

Max almost flinched. That wasn't a pile of umbrellas at The Penguin's feet. It was a whole arsenal!

But Max hadn't gotten where he was today by falling apart in front of his adversaries. If he was going to get out of this, he had to talk to The Penguin as an equal, even if it was monster to monster.

"Frankly," he said firmly, "I think that reputation is a bum rap. I'm a businessman. Tough, yes. Shrewd, okay. But that doesn't make me a monster—"

"Don't embarrass yourself, Max," The Penguin interrupted. "I know all about you. What you hide, I discover. What you put in your toilet, I put on my mantel." He smiled and patted his rotund belly. "Get the picture?"

He had what Max put in his toilet? Max supposed that was one advantage of living in the sewers. But just how literally was he supposed to take this guy?

The Penguin picked up another umbrella and opened it, showing a bright spiral design. It looked sort of like those "hypno-disks" Max used to see in comics and magazines when he was a boy.

And he was worried about some freak who used this kind of gimmick? Max couldn't help but be a little condescending. "What," he asked, "is that supposed to hypnotize me?"

"No," The Penguin replied jovially, "just give you a splitting headache."

"Well," Max replied with gathering confidence, "it's not working."

The Penguin grinned as he pointed the head of the umbrella at the businessman. There was an explosion as Max saw a spout of flame come from the umbrella's barrel.

A gunshot! Max clutched at his chest. Had he been hit?

"You big baby!" The Penguin chided as he waved the umbrella. "Just blanks. Would I go to all this trouble tonight *just* to kill you? No, I have an entirely *other* purpose.''

With that remark, all trace of mirth disappeared from The Penguin's countenance. He looked serious, solemn, almost respectable.

''I'm ready, Max,'' he continued, his voice much less assured than before. ''I've been lingering down here too long.'' He sighed. ''I'm starting to like the smell. Bad sign.''

He looked into Max's eyes with his own beady orbs. ''It's high time for me to ascend. To reemerge. With your help, Max, your know-how, your savvy, your acumen.''

He paused and looked to his circus cronies, who appeared genuinely moved by his admissions.

''I wasn't born in a sewer, you know. I come from—'' He looked up toward some place far above their current location. ''Like you,'' The Penguin continued forcefully. ''And, like you, I want some respect—a recognition of my basic humanity—an occasional breeze!''

A couple of the circus gang seemed on the verge of tears.

''Most of all,'' The Penguin went on, his own voice almost breaking, ''I want to find out who I am. By finding my parents. Learning my human name. Simple stuff that the good people of Gotham take for granted!''

Max still couldn't see this. ''And exactly why am I going to help you?''

The Penguin held out his hand. One of his cronies gave him what must have once been a bright red Christmas stocking, before it got covered by greenish gunk. Oddly enough, it was exactly the same size and shape as those stockings that Max's aged grandmother had knitted for their mantel.

No, Shreck thought. It was a coincidence that this particular stocking looked so familiar. There was a name stitched on the stocking. He had to squint to make it out beneath the grime. The name was "Max."

"Well," The Penguin explained, "let's start with a batch of toxic waste from your *clean* textile plant." He pulled a rusty Thermos from the stocking and unscrewed the cap. "There's a whole lagoon of this crud in the back—"

He poured out a thick goo from the Thermos onto the ice-covered table. The goo sizzled where it hit.

Who did this guy think he was trying to blackmail?

"Yawn," Max replied in great disinterest. "That could have come from anywhere."

"What about the documents that prove you own half the firetraps in Gotham?"

Max raised a single bored eyebrow. "If there were such documents—and that is not an admission—I would have seen to it that they were shredded."

The Penguin again held out his hand. This time, one of the circus goons gave him a stack of something shiny. Max stared. They looked like nothing so much as a stack of shredded papers stuck together with a vast quantity of transparent tape.

"A lot of tape and a little patience make all the difference," The Penguin remarked proudly. "By the way, how's Fred Adkins, your old partner?"

Max could feel his cool slipping away.

"Fred," he murmured.

Anyone could find out about his chemical plant.

"Fred?" he asked nonchalantly.

And it looked like this guy might have reassembled a couple of embarrassing documents.

But how could he know about Fred?

"He's—uh—" Max managed at last, "actually, he's been on an extended vacation, and—"

The Penguin nodded happily and reached under the icy table. He pulled out what looked like a human hand, severed at the wrist.

"Hi, Max!" The Penguin continued, talking from the side of his mouth like some bad ventriloquist. "Remember me? I'm Fred's hand!"

But, Max thought, how could he have that? The hand should have been disposed of!

He caught himself. Just like the chemical waste should have been flushed away, and the shredded papers should have been incinerated. The Penguin obviously was the master of Max's refuse. And he looked like he might be the master of Max's life.

The Penguin leaned toward Max. "Want to greet any other body parts? Or stroll down memory lane with torn-up, kinky Polaroids? Failed urine tests? Remember, Max. You flush it, I flaunt it!"

As cold as it was down here, Max found himself sweating. He did his best to smile.

"You know what, Mr. Penguin, sir?" he asked in his best business voice. "I think perhaps I *could* help orchestrate a little welcome-home scenario for you. And once we're both back home, perhaps we can scratch each other's backs.''

That seemed to please the birdman greatly. ''You won't regret this, Mr. Shreck.'' The Penguin put out his hand.

Max grabbed it and did his best to shake it heartily. But not only did The Penguin's hand look pasty and peculiar, it was also as cold as death.

The Penguin stepped back, but Max still held the hand. He looked down at what he held.

It wasn't The Penguin's hand. It was Fred's.

The circus gang laughed as if this were the funniest thing in the world. Max gingerly let go of the hand and let it fall to the table.

After a minute, Max laughed, too, like his life depended on it.

CHAPTER Twelve

Max was back in the open, out in Gotham Plaza, just like he had been the day before. Except that everything had changed. The businessman smiled and waved to the crowd, and prayed that everything went according to plan.

This time, there wasn't much of a crowd beyond a few curiosity seekers. The smaller stores here had all been trashed. Even Shreck's Department Store had sustained some damage. For now, the shoppers would have to go elsewhere. But in their place were all the TV news-cams with their crews and well-groomed on-the-spot reporters.

And the Mayor was here as well. That was one thing you could depend on with His Honor the Mayor; he never missed a photo opportunity. And when Max suggested that the Mayor might bring his wife and infant son along so that he could make a point about family safety, His Honor had leapt at the suggestion. So it was that Max solemnly walked beside the Mayor and his family, all four of them caught in the glow of TV lights, while the Mayor talked at never-ending length to reporters, and Max waited to see if all this would work. They paused before the speaker's platform.

"I tell you this," the Mayor was currently remarking in the most committed of tones, "not just as an official, but as a husband and father." He raised a warning finger above his head to drive home his point. "Last night's eruption of lawlessness will never happ—"

An acrobat somersaulted from behind the ravaged Christmas tree, straight for the Mayor's wife, snatching the baby from her arms with a single fluid motion. The circus performer leapt back onto the platform, and held the baby aloft as if he were accepting an award.

"I'm not one for speeches," he remarked with a broad grin, "so I'll just say 'Thanks!' "

The Mayor lunged for the acrobat, who calmly kicked His Honor in the chest. His Honor crumpled as the acrobat jumped from the platform and raced through the astonished crowd until—

He catapulted himself into an open manhole.

Max pushed his way forward as the crowd gathered around the dark hole in the street. There was a moment of silence, then noise erupted from below.

"Hey!" someone yelled from down below. "Oww! Get away! Ouch!" The cries of pain were accompanied by a heavy thumping sound, as if someone was being soundly thrashed.

The crowd gasped as the acrobat, battered and bruised with clothing torn, dragged himself from the manhole and ran rather unsteadily—but still very quickly—away through the throng.

No one thought to stop him. He no longer held the baby. And there was something else down in that manhole.

"Stand back!" someone in the crowd yelled.

"My God, look!" another voice cried.

For, out of the darkness, the Mayor's child was being raised up into the light. The crowd gasped. How could such a thing be? It was almost magic. But no, he was being held aloft by someone—or something.

A flipper emerged from the manhole, followed by the portly visage of The Penguin!

The crowd cheered.

The Penguin smiled.

Max had to admit, it couldn't have gone better if he had planned it himself.

Which, after all, he had.

Alfred had paused in his hanging of ornaments on the tree. It was obvious from his expression that he didn't believe this. But then, Bruce Wayne didn't believe it either.

"This morning's miracle," the man on the screen intoned solemnly. "Gotham will never forget."

The TV showed the abduction of the Mayor's baby, and the supposed miracle of his rescue by The Penguin, who rose out of the sewer on top of the strangest of vehicles, a contraption that looked like nothing so much as a large rubber duck. The camera zoomed in on the rescuer.

"That's him," the announcer continued as if he saw large duck vehicles every day. "The shadowy, much rumored penguin man of the sewers, arisen. Until today, he'd been another tabloid myth, alongside the Abominable Snowman and the Loch Ness Monster."

The Mayor's wife was in tears as she grabbed her baby back. She swallowed hard, but somehow managed to embrace the man, or whatever it was, called The Penguin, who certainly looked as if he had spent his life in the sewers, and no doubt smelled accordingly. The Penguin, for his part, blinked as if he could not get used to the brightness of the light.

"But now," the announcer again remarked, "this bashful man-beast can proudly take his place alongside our own legendary Batman."

The Mayor reached out to shake The Penguin's hand. But somehow, Max Shreck had gotten in the way, and now stood beaming by The Penguin, patting him heartily on the back.

"Gotham's leading citizen, Max Shreck," the announcer droned on, "had been on a fact-finding mission in Gotham Plaza."

Shreck bent down to whisper something encouraging in The Penguin's ear. The Penguin, embarrassed, took a little bow. The crowd cheered wildly. Loudspeakers in the plaza began to play "Joy to the World."

The TV picture shifted to a live interview with the new

hero. The Penguin shielded his eyes with a small, frayed umbrella as he spoke in a shy and halting voice:

"All I want in return"—he blinked at the camera—"is the chance to—to find my folks. Find out who they are—and thusly, who I am—and, then, *with* my parents, just—try to understand why"—he paused to take a ragged breath—"why they did what I guess they *had* to do, to a child who was born a little—different. A child who spent his first Christmas, and many since, in a sewer."

His parents, Bruce thought.

Mother. Father. A scream. A gunshot. Lost to him forever.

"Mr. Wayne," Alfred remarked softly. "Is something wrong?"

Bruce looked up to where the butler had returned to trimming the tree. Bruce shook his head, as much to clear it as to indicate the negative.

"No, nothing," he began, "ah—his parents—I—" He took a deep breath. "I hope he finds them."

Alfred heartily agreed as he returned to his tree-trimming duties. Bruce turned back to the television. So The Penguin had lost his mother and father. Or maybe, his mother and father had lost him.

Max smiled most pleasantly from where he stood within the entryway of the Gotham Hall of Records. A short flight of steps beyond, a whole cordon of police held back dozens of reporters, hungry for a story.

"What do you think he'll do to his mom and dad when he finds them?" a reporter asked near the door.

"What would you do to your ma and pa," another reporter replied sarcastically, "if they flushed you down the poop-chute?"

Somehow, one of the reporters had gotten around the cordon, and was quietly mounting the steps. Max snapped his fingers, and a pair of his personal Shreck security guards stepped by him to intercept the intruder.

They grabbed the reporter by the elbows.

"Mr. Penguin is not to be disturbed," one of the guards remarked as he turned the reporter back down the steps.

"The Hall of Records is a public place!" the reporter yelled back in professional outrage. "You're violating the First Amendment, abridging the freedom of the press—"

This had gone far enough. Max waved for his own phalanx of reporters to follow him outside. Now he'd give them the story he'd promised.

As he stepped forward, he waved to the guards to let their escort stay on the steps for the moment.

"What about the freedom to rediscover your roots," Max asked the angry reporter as all the other newsmen around him jotted down his every word, "with dignity, in privacy?"

The once angry reporter smiled. He sensed a story.

"What's the deal, Mr. Shreck?" He thrust his handheld tape recorder straight at Max. "Is The Penguin a personal friend?"

"Yes," Max replied soberly, "he's a personal friend— of this whole city. So have a heart, buddy." He reached forward and hit the stop button on the reporter's recorder. "And give the Constitution a rest, okay? It's Christmas."

* * *

There were so many records, so much to do.

The Penguin sat at a great table in the cavernous main hall of the records building, surrounded by hundreds of thousands of birth certificates. And The Penguin had to look at every one.

Occasionally, he would find what he wanted, and jot it down on a legal pad. He was only vaguely aware of the noises outside, of a crowd of reporters shouting questions and calling his name. This work was far too important to be distracted by such common concerns.

But day ended, and as the night descended, the reporters left at last. Still, The Penguin worked by the light of a single lamp, flipping through the certificates, and jotting down names, boys' names, on his legal pads. He had already filled a tall stack of these pads with names, but his work was not yet done.

After all, this was only the beginning of The Penguin's revenge.

CHAPTER
Thirteen

It was far too quiet.

He guided the Batmobile down the deserted streets of Gotham City. Over the past couple of days, there had been almost a complete halt in heavy-duty crime; not a single bank heist, only one bungled attempt to hold up a convenience store, hardly even any murders. It was as if the criminals of Gotham City were staying off the streets, waiting for something really big.

A light flashed on the console in front of him. Alfred was calling. Batman pressed a button, and the butler's face lit up a small video screen by the wheel.

"The city's been noticeably quiet since the thwarted baby-napping, yet still you patrol," Alfred announced in that disapproving way he had. "What about eating? Sleeping? You won't be much good to anyone else if you don't look after yourself.''

''The Red Triangle Circus Gang'' was Batman's terse reply. ''They're jackals, Alfred. They hunt in packs, at night—''

He glanced out the windshield. He had almost reached his destination.

''Are you concerned about that strange heroic Penguin person?'' Alfred asked in his dry British manner.

Batman laughed. He pulled the Batmobile up in front of the Gotham Hall of Records. Two men, a policeman and a Shreck security guard, stood to either side of the entryway, or, to be more accurate, they slumped, since both appeared to be dozing.

Batman looked up at the single lit window within the hall. Why was The Penguin still inside?

''Funny you should ask, Alfred,'' he said to the butler. ''Maybe I am a bit concerned.''

Well, now, this was quite a turnout. Not only was the press out in force—but then, these days, they followed The Penguin everywhere—but there was a huge crowd of the general public as well, including a small number of young women dressed in black. Who were they? Penguin groupies? If he had known this sort of thing was going to happen, he would have come out of the sewers sooner. Now, if he could only determine some way that he could show his appreciation for these fine, nubile young women without the press nosing around. Ah well. All things in their time. At this moment, he had other fish to swallow.

The police once again formed a living chain to keep the

curious away as The Penguin strode forward onto the tiny, private cemetery plot tucked in a forgotten corner of Gotham. The well-manicured headstone he sought was immediately ahead, with separate inscriptions for Tucker and Esther Cobblepot, his very dearly departed father and mother. It was a shame that they both had to die so young. And so mysteriously.

The Penguin fell to his knees in front of the markers, and reached within one frayed sleeve to pull out a pair of roses that, frankly, were a little the worse for wear. Oh, well, no matter. It was the sentiment that counted. And, by The Penguin's count, there were at least a dozen TV and film cameras recording this sentiment at this very moment. And there was no way anyone could ever count all the news cameras.

The Penguin stood, and thought he saw a couple of his groupies swoon at the great emotion of his actions. Ah, yes, he would like to get one or two of those little chicks alone. But not here. Not now.

Instead, he walked back toward the crowd of reporters. One obnoxious example of the profession pushed forward from his fellows.

"So," the reporter began, "Mr. Penguin—"

The Penguin held up his umbrella in protest. "A 'penguin' is a bird that cannot fly," he remarked sternly yet sadly. "I am a man. I have a name. It's Oswald Cobblepot." Or at least it was now his name whenever it suited him.

"Mr. Cobblepot!" the reporter continued, unfazed. He waved toward the grave of The Penguin's parents. "You'll never get a chance to settle with them, huh?"

The crowd gasped at the effrontery of the reporter. My, The Penguin thought, it was certainly good to have the masses on his side. He twirled his umbrella pensively for a moment before he replied.

"True, I was their number one son"—he glanced back pensively at the twin headstones—"and they treated me like number two. But it's human nature to fear the unusual—even with all their education and privilege. My dad, a district attorney, mother active in the DAR; perhaps, when I held my Tiffany baby rattle with a shiny flipper, they freaked."

He paused and turned to the crowd before he continued.

"But I forgive them."

The crowd cheered one more time. He had them in the palm of his hand.

Or should that be the palm of his flipper?

All of Gotham City was talking about The Penguin.

"Penguin forgives parents!" the paperboy called. "Read all about it! 'I'm fully at peace with myself and the world!' Get your paper!"

And Gotham City responded, grabbing the newsprint as soon as the papers could be dropped from the trucks. Everybody stopped whatever they were doing to read the charming news.

" 'You don't need hands as long as you've got heart,' " quoted one from the paper before him.

" 'My heart is filled with love,' " a second read aloud. " 'I feel five feet tall.' "

"He's like a frog," another exclaimed, "that became a prince!"

"No, actually he's more like a penguin," another, calmer head replied.

A couple passed nearby, talking as animatedly as everyone else. "Abandoned penguins from the old Arctic World raised him!"

"Makes you remember the true meaning of the holiday," the woman chimed in. "The love, the giving—"

Max chuckled. He'd been in that Arctic World, that old leftover pavilion from some world's fair or wonders-of-tomorrow technology exhibition. Max should probably read a paper to find out which one. There used to be a lot of that sort of thing around Gotham City, back when ordinary people had money.

But that same pavilion was The Penguin's hideout now, and the place where he hid the Red Triangle Circus Gang. The main thing Max remembered about the place was the smell.

Still, the way the Gothamites were grabbing papers, his plan had worked, and then some. He just hoped that The Penguin would be sufficiently grateful when the time came. After all, Max might be rich—but he could always get richer.

Bruce Wayne had some reading to do.

He studied the front page of the newspaper projected on the video screen before him; the page was old and yellowed but still very readable. He had installed this special computerized microfiche reader in the Batcave for just this sort of instant access to history.

He pressed a button on the console before him. The reader jumped to the next page.

" 'Red Triangle Circus put on a swell show last night, with fierce lions . . . ' " he read aloud from the screen before him. No, there was nothing of value in this article. He quickly hit the correct combination of keys, and the command appeared at the top of the screen: CONTINUE SEARCH FOR: RED TRIANGLE.

He waited a few seconds as back issues blurred by before another paper came into focus.

" 'Triangle Circus has returned for a two-week . . .' " Bruce read, " '. . . kids will love . . .' "

It was still too early in the circus's career, before they had turned to a life of crime, or, more likely, before the police had discovered it.

He hit the search key again as Alfred entered the room. The butler had brought him his supper on a tray.

"Thanks, Alfred," Bruce murmured as the butler placed the tray upon a table by his side. Alfred smiled and nodded his reply.

Bruce picked up a spoon and took a sip of the soup. He blinked in surprise.

"It's cold," he told Alfred.

The butler nodded again, as if this news was no surprise to him. "It's vichyssoise, sir."

Bruce looked at the soup before him. "Vichyssoise." Oh. "Supposed to be cold, right?" Foolish of him to think Alfred might have made a mistake. But he had to get back to his search.

"Mr. Wayne," Alfred remarked gently. "Does the phrase 'Christmas holiday' hold any resonance for you?"

Bruce laughed. He grabbed one of the data-coded CDs

from his desk and lobbed it to the other man, letting it sail through the air like a Frisbee.

"Listen to yourself, Alfred," he told the butler. "Hassling me yesterday, in my car."

Alfred dutifully placed the CD in a nearby player. An instant later, he could hear his own voice:

"What about eating? Sleeping? You won't be much good to anyone else if—"

Bruce picked up the remote and turned the player off.

"I learned to live without a mother a long time ago, thanks," he added. Alfred raised an eyebrow, but did not otherwise respond.

Very well, Bruce thought. If he couldn't get the old fellow to listen to reason, he would simply ignore him. He turned back to his reading.

" 'Triangle Circus is back,' " he read aloud, " 'With a freak show that may not be suitable for your kids, featuring a bearded lady, the world's fattest man, and an aquatic bird boy.' "

He turned to Alfred in triumph. There it was. Exactly the sort of thing he was looking for.

Alfred still did not appear impressed. "Why are you now determined to prove that this Penguin—er, Mr. Cobblepot—is not what he seems? Must you be the only lonely 'man-beast' in town?"

Bruce's only answer was to read a choice part of the next article aloud:

" '. . . Circus folded its tents yesterday, perhaps forever. After numerous reports of missing children in several towns, police have closed down the Red Triangle's fairgrounds. However, at least one freak-show performer vanished before he could be questioned.' ''

There! Alfred had to see the connection now. Bruce turned to his servant with a triumphant grin.

"I suppose you feel better now, sir," Alfred remarked dryly.

Did he? Bruce thought about it. What satisfaction would he get from information that The Penguin was probably a vicious criminal plotting something against Gotham City? It certainly wasn't reassuring.

"No," Bruce admitted, "actually I feel worse."

The two men regarded each other for a long moment in silence. After all, what else could be said?

Alfred frowned at his employer.

"Eat your vichyssoise," he instructed.

CHAPTER
Fourteen

One way or another, Selina would finish this. Unless it finished her first. Her pen sped across the page of the pad in front of her. She already had twelve other pages of notes that she had made from the computer files, and all those pages were in shorthand. She was almost done, though. One more file to browse through, and then she could go back over her notes to see if they made any sense.

Her pen stopped, and so did her heart, when she felt a hand on her shoulder. She looked up to see Max grinning down at her. This late at night? Something must be wrong. Max Slavemaster never worked after six.

"Working late?" Max asked solicitously. "I'm touched."

"No," Selina replied under her breath, "I am." She quickly added in her official executive assistant voice, "Well, I'm boning up for your Bruce Wayne meeting in the morning."

Max still didn't look convinced. He never realized how hard she worked. Well, this time she would tell him, in every gory detail.

"I pulled all the files on the proposed power plant," she continued, "and Mr. Wayne's hoped-for investment." She pointed to the pages of shorthand in front of her. "I've studied up on all of it. I even opened the protected files and—"

For the first time since she had begun her description, Max looked impressed.

"Why, how industrious," he remarked with a smile. "And how did you open protected files, may I ask?"

"Well," Selina replied, glad to be on her boss's good side for a change, "I figured that your password was 'Finster.' Your Chihuahua. And it was." People always used the names of kids and pets as passwords; it was one of the first things you learned as an administrative assistant.

She glanced back at her notes again. "And it's all very interesting, though a bit on the technical side, I mean how the power plant is a power plant in name only since in fact it's going to be one giant—"

What was the word? She glanced up at Max, but he only gave her a nod of encouragement.

"A big giant *capacitor*," she continued as soon as she found the reference. "And that, instead of generating power, it'll sort of be"—this is where her notes, or the concepts behind them, started to get confusing—"*sucking* power from Gotham City and storing it—stockpiling it, sort of? Which is a very novel approach, I'd say.''

She looked back up to her boss.

''And who,'' he replied smoothly, ''would you say this to?''

With that, he calmly lit a match and set fire to her notes.

Selina swallowed. Perhaps she had overstepped her authority.

''Well,'' she replied, hoping for the right answer, ''—um—nobody?''

Max dropped the burning notepad into the trash. Selina did not like his current smile one bit.

''What did curiosity do to the cat?'' Max asked much too gently. He took a step toward her.

''I'm no cat,'' Selina replied quickly, although at the moment she wished she could be as small, and as swift, as one. ''I'm just an assistant,'' she added. Totally unimportant. Pay no attention to little old me. ''A secretary—''

''And a very, very good one,'' Max agreed as he continued his approach.

''Too good?'' Selina guessed.

Max nodded all too readily. Why was this the time, after all those screwups, that she had to be right?

Selina took a step away. ''It's our secret,'' she said brightly. ''Honest. How can you be so mean to someone so meaningless?''

''The power plant is to be my pyramid,'' Max replied with a chilling conviction. ''My cathedral, my legacy to Chip. Nothing must prevent that.''

Selina's back hit the plate-glass window. There was nowhere else for her to go. But Max kept on coming.

This was all too much, Selina thought. She was about to get frightened half out of her skull. Who did this Shreck guy think he was, after all?

"Okay," she said, trying to sound firm, "go ahead. Intimidate me. Bully me, if it makes you feel big. I mean, it's not like you can just kill me!"

Max shook his head sadly. "Actually, it's a lot like that."

Selina stared at him. What did he mean by that?

Max smiled.

Selina wiped a tear of fright from her cheek. What a relief.

"For a second," she said to Max, "you really frightened—"

Max grabbed her and savagely pushed her through the plate glass.

CHAPTER
Fifteen

S he was falling. Down through the darkness and the swirling snow. It was so beautiful. If you had to die, maybe this was the way to do it.

She heard canvas rip as she fell through an awning. She couldn't feel anything anymore. Then she hit a second awning, and a third, all the fronts of the fancy multistoried Gotham Plaza. They had slowed her fall, but—

She was surrounded by cold, and white. She must have fallen into snow. She had no breath left in her.

"Help me—" she managed. "Somebody—" Someone warm and loving, someone above all this.

"Miss Kitty—" she called.

Her world went from white to black.

* * *

What had he done?

The power plant was important to him and his future plans, certainly. Free electric power would be indispensable in his plans to undercut his competitors, especially as foreign investment drove this country to its collective knees. No matter who won that battle, the Shrecks would survive.

But perhaps he felt too strongly about that survival, to do something like this. Max shivered as he looked out the remains of the window. He would have to concoct a story. And they would certainly have to do something about the broken glass.

He turned and saw Chip standing in the doorway. Max would have to come up with a story even sooner than he had thought.

"It—it was terrible," he stumbled. "I leaned over—and accidentally knocked her—out—"

Chip nodded sympathetically. "She jumped," he corrected his father. "She'd been depressed."

Max stared at his son for an instant before he realized what was going on. "Yes. *Yes*," he agreed heartily. That was it exactly. "Boyfriend trouble?" he suggested.

Chip shook his head. "P.M.S.," he stated decisively. He turned and walked from the room.

Max could only stare after him in admiration. Now *there* was a son!

There are certain things that go beyond rational explanation. One of them is the connection felt sometimes between two spirits, lovers, perhaps, who can sense each other's thoughts when they are apart; or a parent who knows something has happened to a child half a world away. But these connections are not limited to humans alone.

Sometimes, at moments of extreme stress or peril, they are even shared between human and animal. Master and pet, if you will, although the real dynamic is far more complicated than that.

The woman who was Selina Kyle would have these thoughts later, after she was rescued.

At that moment, though, she lay half-conscious, battered and bruised and about to freeze to death in the snow. It would be so easy, she thought, to drift off to sleep, and maybe to sleep forever.

Something kept her from falling into that final sleep. There were noises, animal noises. The sound of cats.

Miss Kitty?

But it was far more than one cat. From all the meows and purrs that surrounded her, she must be in the middle of an army of cats, as if the whole feline population of Gotham City had come to her rescue.

That was awfully nice of them. She had always liked cats. Now, if they would only calm down so she could get some sleep.

But the cats wouldn't leave her alone. Miss Kitty climbed upon her chest and breathed into her mouth. A Siamese purred meaningfully into her ear. Other cats rubbed against her legs and feet.

An old tom bit her finger.

Her eyes flew open.

And she understood. She was Selina Kyle no more. She was reborn.

CHAPTER
Sixteen

It seemed to take hours to get back to her apartment. Her bruises no longer mattered, nor her loss of blood, nor even the cold of the winter night. She would never again be a meek, self-deprecating administrative assistant.

She entered her apartment with Miss Kitty in hand, but this place no longer suited her mood; it didn't speak of her awakening. There would have to be a few changes to this place.

So she set to work, with black spray paint, ending the pink and eggshell decor of walls and floor and couch. It was still not enough. She grabbed her stuffed animals and fed the smaller ones to the garbage disposal. The larger ones had to be done in with knives. A knitting needle effectively ruined the perfect order of the dollhouse.

And, after that, she used some interesting black scraps to sew a very special outfit. And claws; she needed claws! Well, why not make them from common household implements? It was amazing how easily things found around the kitchen could be turned into deadly weapons.

Miss Kitty roamed about the apartment, full of purrs and imperious meows, approving of every change.

Now, there was one final task. With her bare hands, she tore at the cheerful neon sign, removing those two most crucial letters, so that what once read "HELLO THERE" was transformed to something much more appropriate:

"HELL HERE."

For it would be hell for all those who had wronged her.

With that, she sat down upon the floor in her new, special clothes, and watched the sunrise, for her work had taken the rest of the night. Miss Kitty purred at her feet. She thought the cat deserved a little reward after so much work, and fetched her a bowl full of milk. She placed the bowl before her feline savior and expressed herself for the first time in a new voice that spoke of a power and grace she had never admitted to in her earlier life.

"I don't know about you, Miss Kitty," she said softly but firmly, "but I feel—so—much—yummier."

And with that, she stretched out to reach the rising sun; stretched out just like a cat.

Bruce Wayne moved quickly through Gotham Plaza. It was still a mess. A group of workmen forlornly tried to shore up a bullet-ridden Christmas tree that seemed obviously beyond saving, while others boarded up the windows of the burnt-out stores. He knew some of those places wanted to open before Christmas. Right now, it looked hopeless.

Bruce stepped forward to shake hands. He also took this opportunity to study the window more closely.

"Hmm," he grunted. "Primitive ventilation."

"Damn those Carny Bolsheviks the other night," Max responded quickly, "throwing bricks at my window—"

"No," Bruce disagreed. He pointed to the evidence on the carpet. Or rather the lack of evidence. "No glass on the inside."

Max frowned at the carpet, looking a little uncomfortable. "Weird, huh?" he said after a moment. "Uh, why don't we go into the conference room?"

"It's less well ventilated," Chip added helpfully.

Bruce agreed and allowed Max to lead the way. They stepped through a second doorway into a room dominated by a large, circular conference table. Max indicated that Bruce should take a seat. Once his guest was seated, the businessman sat down at the opposite side of the table.

"I'd offer you coffee," he explained hurriedly, "but my assistant is using her vacation time."

"Good time, too," Bruce agreed. He pursed his lips as he added, "Everyone but the bandits seem to be slacking off until New Year's."

Max turned to stare at Bruce. "Not sure I like the inference, Bruce," he said with a smile. "I'm pushing this power plant now because it'll cost more later." He shook an authoritative finger in Bruce's direction. "Time is money, life is short, and a million saved is a million earned."

Bruce snapped open the briefcase that he had set down

on the conference table. "I commissioned this report," he announced matter-of-factly. "Thought you should see it."

He handed it to Max, who flipped through it as if he really wasn't interested.

Bruce had had enough of this playing around. "Here's the point, Max," he said candidly. "Gotham City has a power surplus. I'm sure you know that. So the question is, What's your angle?"

Max jumped back to his feet. " 'A power *surplus*'?" he exclaimed as if those were dirty words. "Bruce, shame on you—no such thing! One can never have too much power!"

Chip, standing behind his father, rapidly nodded his agreement.

"If my life has any meaning," Max insisted, "that's the meaning."

"Max," Bruce replied firmly, "I'm gonna fight you on this. The mayor and I have already spoken and we see eye to eye here. So—"

"Mayors come and go," Max shot back. "And heirs tire easily." He put up his dukes and threw a punch at the air. "Really think a flyweight like you could last fifteen rounds with Muhammad Shreck?"

"Guess we'll find out, Max," Bruce agreed noncommittally. "Of course, I don't have a crime boss like Cobblepot in my corner."

He shut his briefcase and stood.

"Crime boss?" Max shouted. He laughed harshly. "Shows what you know, Mr. To-the-manor-born-with-a-silver-spoon. Oswald is Gotham's new Golden Boy!"

"Oswald controls the Red Triangle Circus Gang,"

Bruce shot back. "I can't prove it, but we both know it's true."

"Wayne," Max insisted, "I'll not stand for mud-slinging in this office. If my assistant were here, she'd already have escorted you out, to—"

"Wherever he wants," a female voice interrupted.

Bruce turned to see a woman enter the room. And what a woman. She was very fashionably dressed, with a haircut that framed and highlighted her face. The only thing out of place was a bandage on her hand. She was very attractive, and also somehow familiar.

"Preferably some nightspot, grotto, or secluded hideaway," she continued as she sashayed into the room. She smiled at Bruce. "Nice suit."

Of course! Bruce thought. They had met in Gotham Plaza the other day. She was that same woman the clown had seized as a hostage. She had seemed so uncertain, then, compared with the way she looked at him now.

Their eyes had met for an instant the other day. She looked nice then. Their eyes met again. She looked even nicer now.

Bruce smiled back.

"Selina?" Max looked as if he had seen a ghost. "Selina—Selina—" He sounded like an old record, stuck in a single groove.

"That's my name, Maxamillions," the woman replied with the slightest of smiles. "Don't wear it out, babe, or I'll make you buy me a new one."

Max blinked and shook his head, as if to clear it of errant thoughts. "Uh—Selina, this is—uh—Bruce Wayne."

"We've met," Bruce replied suavely.

Selina looked the slightest bit confused. "Have we?"

Bruce's smile faltered as he realized that she hadn't met him at all. She had met Batman.

"Sorry," he said quickly. "I mistook me for somebody else."

"You mean mistook *me*?" Selina corrected.

"Didn't I say that?" Bruce asked.

"Yes and no," she replied with another of those fabulous smiles. But her hand was bandaged. Bruce stepped forward and gently took that hand with his own.

"What happened?" he asked.

"Yes, did—" Max hurriedly interrupted, "did you injure yourself on that ski slope? Is that why you cut short your vacation and came back?" He smiled at her. Somehow, Bruce thought, the smile did not look at all pleasant.

Selina shrugged with the slightest of frowns. "Maybe that broken window over there had something to do with it—or maybe not. It's blurry." She bit her lip slightly. Bruce thought she looked even better when she bit her lip.

"I mean," she continued after a moment's pause, "it's not complete amnesia." She frowned, then continued tentatively. "I—remember Sister Mary-Margaret puking in church, and Becky Riley said it was morning sickness." Her smile returned as she talked. "And I remember the time I forgot to wear underpants to school, and the name of the boy who noticed—Ricky Friedberg!" Her smile had transformed into the largest of grins. "He's dead now." She glanced at Max. "But last night?" She shook her head. "Complete and total blur."

Max still smiled, although now the expression seemed

a little frightened. "Selina," he remarked as he glanced at his son. "Please show out Mr. Wayne."

Selina smiled at Bruce again and turned to lead him to the elevator. Bruce decided he could follow her anywhere. But the elevators were only two short rooms away. Much too short to have any sort of meaningful conversation.

Selina turned to him once they were both out in the hall. "You don't seem like the type that does business with Mr. Shreck," she said frankly.

"No," Bruce agreed. "And you don't seem like the type to take orders from him."

There was that smile again. "Well, that's a—long story."

"Well," Bruce volunteered. "I could free up some time."

Selina gazed into his eyes.

"I'm listed."

Bruce gazed back into hers.

"I'm tempted."

Selina took a step back toward the conference room.

"I'm working."

Bruce took a step away toward the elevators.

"I'm leaving."

She disappeared, back into the offices of Max Shreck and Company. Bruce turned to the elevator.

"Se—li—na," he murmured.

He pressed the down button once for each syllable.

The car arrived. She was listed. He stepped inside. He'd have to give her a call. Except—

He leapt forward, forcing the doors apart before they could close completely.

He was missing the most important information of all.

The woman who was once Selina had taken off her bandage, and slowly, methodically, was squeezing blood from her finger into the percolating coffee.

So, Max. Want some more of my blood?

She looked up, and saw Bruce Wayne watching her.

She tried to smile.

"Pouring myself into my work," she explained.

Bruce smiled back. "I, ah, didn't catch your last name."
Just like that. As if he saw people dripping blood into coffee every day.

"Oh," she replied. "Kyle."

She put her left hand to her ear, and made an exaggerated circling motion with her right index finger. "Rhymes with *dial*."

97

He gave her a thumbs-up and disappeared.

There was something about that man, she thought. Something that almost made her want to go back to being plain old Selina Kyle.

She purred deep in her throat. Almost, but not quite.

Max had to admit it. This Selina thing had him spooked. Her death would have been so much simpler. But he couldn't let this little setback destroy his confidence.

It was time to call The Penguin, and check up on Oswald's new home. Not, of course, that Oswald Cobblepot knew anything about its real purpose. Yet.

Chip looked at him as he picked up the phone.

"You buy this 'blurry' business?" his son asked.

"Who knows," Max replied as he began to dial the number. "Women." He glanced back up at his son, and he finished dialing. The phone on the other end began to ring.

A gruff voice answered.

"Yeah," Max replied into the receiver. "Oswald, please."

His son waved in agreement and left the room as Max waited for The Penguin.

This would work out fine.

The phone rang in The Penguin's warehouse.

Oswald Cobblepot had to admit it; Max had come through on this one. His new headquarters had two different floors. Downstairs was big and brightly lit and still under construction, as if Max was planning to give The

Penguin some sort of office. No doubt it would be a good place to meet the public, if The Penguin ever wanted to do that sort of thing.

Upstairs, it was a different story: dirty, dingy, cluttered—a real working space. The Red Triangle Circus Gang hung out up here, practicing their acts and generally acting rowdy. They had opened a large ventilation duct up here that also opened up at the rear of the building, so that the gang members could come and go at will without the embarrassment of having to deal with those boringly legitimate people on the first floor.

And The Penguin had his list of names, all on that pile of yellow legal pads. Now all he had to do was cross-reference every single one of them against the white pages of Gotham phone books. It was not a simple job.

The phone kept on ringing.

The Organ Grinder shooed his monkeys away to answer it.

"Yeah?" he said. He held the phone out toward The Penguin. "For you, boss."

Now? The Penguin grabbed the phone and almost growled into the receiver. "Yeah? What is it? I'm busy up here."

"Good," Max's all-too-cheerful voice greeted him on the line. "Stay busy up there. I got plans for us below."

What did he mean? Down at the lower level of his new headquarters? Well, The Penguin supposed since he had made the deal, he had to put up with Max. He never realized how much it would interfere with his work here.

"Plans," he repeated halfheartedly. "Swell. Later."

He slammed down the phone. He'd deal with Max at the proper time. For now, he had to finish off the phone books and his list.

It was a lot of work, but because of this, his final revenge would be that much sweeter. He returned to matching addresses with every single name.

After all, all play and no work made a dull Penguin.

CHAPTER
Eighteen

It was time to prowl.

She could no longer stay in her den, even after it had been transformed. Cats were meant to roam the night.

So she roamed.

What did we have here?

The dirty streets of Gotham seemed to have coughed up some more of their scum. And who is it today? Just your average, garden-variety mugger, who had grabbed a pretty young woman and dragged her back into an alley.

"Help, Batma—" the woman began.

Batman? Is that all the woman could think of?

"Now, now," the mugger smirked, "pretty young thing, nice and easy—"

The victim cowered and held out her purse. "Please. Don't hurt me. I'll do anything—"

The other woman had had quite enough of this.

She leapt from the fire escape, landing squarely on the mugger's back. He flew forward to the ground.

"I just love a big strong man who's not afraid to show it," she mentioned as he rolled beneath her, "with someone half her size."

The mugger had managed to roll onto his back. He stared up at her in astonishment. "Who the—" he began.

"Be gentle," she replied. "It's my first time."

Apparently he wasn't listening, because he leapt up with a growl, intent on grabbing her.

She darted out of the way, and gave him a savage kick. All the breath left him as he staggered back.

Hey, not bad, she thought. But before he could recover, it was time for the talons.

She jumped forward and set to work scratching up his face.

The mugger screamed and fell to the asphalt.

"Tic—tac—toe," she murmured in triumph.

The victim rushed up to her side.

"Thank you," she gushed, "thank you. I was so scared—"

Her defender had had enough of this, too. She pushed the victim back against the wall with one of her claws.

"You make it so easy, don't you?" she asked in disgust. "You pretty, pathetic young thing? Always waiting for some Bat*man* to save you."

The victim cringed again, quaking, expecting something even worse.

She leaned forward to whisper in the victim's ear: "I am Catwoman. Hear me roar."

And with that, Catwoman leapt away, cartwheeling out of the alley to disappear into the night.

CHAPTER
Nineteen

With all these interruptions, The Penguin would never finish!

He looked up to see Max Shreck stepping between the members of the Red Triangle Circus, past the Tatooed Strongman, rippling those belly dancers he had tattooed on his biceps, stopping to let one of the acrobats walk past on his hands. Max grinned at The Penguin. Somehow, he seemed much too cheerful for a businessman.

Max nodded at all the performers around them.

"Ah," he remarked, "your—extended family."

The Penguin sighed. Max was leading up to something. His lists would have to wait for the minute.

"Come on downstairs, Oswald," Max urged. "I have a—surprise."

The Penguin scowled. "I don't like surprises." Sometimes, The Penguin still thought it was a mistake to come out of those sewers.

But Max was insistent. He waved The Penguin away from his desk and toward a spiral stairs.

Hesitantly, The Penguin walked forward. So far, Max had more than held up his part of the bargain. And the businessman certainly knew, should anything happen to The Penguin, his circus friends were very good at revenge.

So this had to be something good.

Still, The Penguin thought of icy waters.

"Don't want to spoil it!" Max explained as he tried to put his hands over the Penguin's eyes.

The Penguin growled. Trusting people was one thing, but *certain* people were asking for it. Max quickly pulled his hands away.

"Then close your eyes," Max insisted.

Oh, all right. The Penguin dutifully closed his eyes almost all the way as Max led him down the stairs. This had *better* be good, or he'd let the circus gang practice on Max even earlier than he had planned.

He opened his eyes when they went from stairs to concrete.

"Ta-da!" Max announced.

The Penguin looked around the storefront. It had been transformed from an old drugstore into something bustling and cheerful, full of brand-new desks and state-of-the-art computers and smiling college kids. The place had gotten a bright white coat of paint, too, after which the walls had been covered with red, white, and blue bunting. But the most astonishing things here were the signs and posters, the biggest of which read COBBLEPOT FOR MAYOR.

As if this wasn't enough, there were posters taped all around, and every one had The Penguin's picture on it, along with the words OZZIE VS. THE INSIDERS!

Everyone cheered and applauded. Max's grin got even bigger.

The Penguin was flabbergasted.

"But—" he began. "What—" he added. "I—I mean—" he tried.

He didn't know what he meant.

What was going on here?

"Yes," Max said effusively, "adulation is a cross to bear. God knows I know. But someone's got to supplant our standing-in-the-way-of-progress mayor, and don't deny it, Mr. Cobblepot, your charisma is bigger than both of us!"

"Mayor?" The Penguin replied.

Max smiled and grinned. "Mayor."

But this didn't make any sense, even to somebody who had lived most of his life in the sewers.

"Max," he pointed out, "elections happen in November. Is this not late December?"

Max waved a well-dressed pair forward; so well-dressed that they smelled of money, and success, and power. One man and one woman, both wearing appropriately dark-colored suits, both smiling perfectly gleaming white smiles.

They made The Penguin nervous.

The man stared critically at The Penguin before his smile returned.

"Keep the umbrella!" he announced. "Works for you! I'm Josh. Here!" He shoved something in The Penguin's mouth. "Reclaim your birthright!"

The Penguin glared down at the new object between his lips. It was a jet-black cigarette holder. The woman was circling him now. The Penguin wished he were back upstairs with his yellow notepads.

"I'm Jen," she announced as she grabbed his sleeve. "Stand still for a second while I slip on these little glove thingies—"

Glove thingies? The Penguin glanced over at her handiwork. She was rather attractive under that suit. And he would certainly like to get under that suit. Her smile turned to a grimace as she touched his flippers. It was, The Penguin guessed, just that special way he had with women.

"Our research tells us that voters like fingers," Jen explained as she slipped on the deep black material.

The Penguin frowned at his new gloves. Still, if women liked fingers rather than flippers—

That Josh person, in the meantime, was fingering The Penguin's coat. Now what was this guy's problem? Sure The Penguin's clothes were worn, certainly they were tattered, and perhaps the fabric had stood so much use that it had turned a bit shiny, but as far as The Penguin was concerned, these clothes were a part of him.

"Not a lot of reflective surfaces down in that sewer, huh?" Josh remarked.

Reflective surfaces? Oh, he meant mirrors. Jen laughed. The Penguin liked the way she laughed. He laughed, too. All the people around them started to laugh as well.

"Still," The Penguin remarked, "it could be worse. My nose could be gushing blood."

Josh frowned at that. "Your nose could? What do you mean?"

So The Penguin bit him, quickly, viciously, right on the nose. Make fun of him, would they? Well, the penguins who had raised him had shown him a trick or two!

"Enough!" Max called, pulling the two combatants apart. "Everyone—"

He waved them all back to work as Josh fainted to the floor. The fellow had no stamina at all. Max would have to get a better grade of consultant than that to keep up with The Penguin!

Max led the short man in black over to a quiet corner.

"You're right," Max admitted when they could not be overheard. "We missed the regularly scheduled election. But elected officials can be recalled, impeached, given the boot! Think of Nixon, Meachem, Barry—" He paused, and pointed to the great banner overhead. "Then think of you, Oswald Cobblepot, filling the void."

But Oswald Cobblepot was still watching Jen. "I'd like to fill *her* void," he murmured.

"We need signatures," Max insisted. "To overturn the ballot. I can supply those, Oswald."

"Teach her my 'French flipper' trick," The Penguin continued. It was amazing, the wonderful things you could learn while working for the circus.

"Oswald," Max persevered. "We need one more thing."

The Penguin blinked. Oh, yes. The Mayor's office; that's what they were talking about, wasn't it?

"A platform?" he suggested. "Let me see. 'Stop Global Warming! Start Global Cooling!' Make the world a giant icebox—"

"That's fine, Oswald," Max agreed all too readily. "But to get the mayor recalled, we still need a catalyst, a trigger, an incident."

Yeah, The Penguin thought, *mayor*. Now that he had gotten used to the idea, he really liked it. He could hear them now.

"You're doing great, Mayor Cobblepot," he said aloud. Yeah. He liked the sound of that. And more than that. "Your table is ready, Mayor Cobblepot." And how about women? Women like Jen? Hey, once he was mayor, he would have his pick of women! "I need you, Oswald. I need you now. That's the biggest parasol I've ever—"

"Like the Reichstag fire," Max continued urgently. "The Gulf of Tonkin."

What was Max saying? Perhaps that The Penguin wasn't mayor quite yet. Okay, he would accept that. After all, he used to do twelve shows a day; he could handle anything.

But there was work to do. Dirty work. And The Penguin knew just who could do it.

"Ah," he suggested. "You want my old friends upstairs to drive the mayor into a foaming frenzy."

Max grinned at that.

"Precisely," he agreed. "But they must always come and go via the plumbing ducts that I've provided."

Then Max was suggesting secret sabotage?

"Sounds like fun," The Penguin agreed. "But I—"

He hesitated. This was all happening so fast, he had almost forgotten his true purpose.

Max looked at him questioningly.

"I mustn't get sidetracked," The Penguin explained. "I've got my own—"

"Sidetracked?" Max interrupted. He threw open his arms to include not only their surroundings but all of Gotham City. "Oswald, this is your chance to fulfill a destiny that your parents carelessly discarded—"

Hey. Max had a point there. What was it that obnoxious pantywaist Josh had said? Oh, yeah.

"Reclaim my birthright, you mean?" The Penguin asked. Now that he thought of it, it sounded pretty good.

Max nodded, arms still opened wide. "Imagine." He closed one fist. "As mayor you'll have the ear of the media." He closed the other fist. "Access to captains of industry." He opened both hands and cupped them before him. "Unlimited poontang!"

The Penguin was impressed. "You drive a hard bargain, Max." He paused only long enough to realize he had made up his mind. "All right. I'll be the mayor."

He turned away from the businessman, and walked over to the windows of the storefront, which were hidden behind a heavy set of blinds. Thrusting his new glove between the slats, he looked out at Gotham City at night; a city that would soon be his. He could have it all—the mayor's office first, and then, with the whole city at his feet, he'd complete his sweet revenge.

The Penguin smiled and whispered three words: "Burn, baby, burn."

CHAPTER
Twenty

Nothing's as good as the circus. And that went double when the circus gang decided it was time to steal.

The Organ Grinder played a merry tune as his monkey danced, then pressed the plunger. Boom went the Insta-Teller Machine! The monkey danced forward to snatch the cash.

"All this dough!" the Organ Grinder exclaimed. "It's burning a hole in my pocket!"

And that was only the beginning. The Fat Clown related every evil deed to The Penguin as it occurred.

"The Ice Rink was torched!" he said in that jolly way of his. Then, with hardly any pause at all, "The Twelfth Precinct reports offensive graffiti and—a pharmacy heist!"

The Penguin made a fist with his new black glove.

"I'd love to get my flippers dirty," he cried in triumph. He threw his fist forward, smacked his lips. "Bust someone's skull. Eat someone's pet—"

Then again, he realized, that might not be the mayoral thing to do.

"But action must be balanced with discretion," he remarked. Ah, the trials of office. At least they wouldn't interfere with his other task.

He returned to the phone books and his legal pads. He had to add some more addresses to his list.

Gotham City was falling apart.

Selina looked out of her window. People ran, she heard three or four different kinds of sirens. There was a fire in the distance. She heard gunshots that sounded like they could have come from around the corner.

Miss Kitty meowed at her.

Why not?

She quickly changed her clothes.

"An orgy of sex and violence?" she said to her cat. "Count me in, Miss Kitty."

She crawled out onto the fire escape. Watch out, Gotham City!

It was time for Catwoman to sharpen her claws.

Violence filled the night.

A woman with a belt filled with knives chose an ax instead to beat down a door. The gang members around her were content to simply beat up defenseless citizens who happened to be passing by.

Batman stepped from the shadows.

And all the thugs turned to greet him.

He reached down to his belt and pulled out a small electronic device that would be perfect for this occasion. He held the box in one hand as he punched four white dots, then a red, with the other hand.

The woman with the knives threw a blade straight into Batman's chest. It lodged in the insignia of his body armor. He'd have to pull it out when he had a free minute. Batman punched in a second code to follow the first.

All the thugs howled as one as they rushed toward him. Batman pressed a final button, and two wings sprouted from the sides of the box. His computerized Batarang was ready to take them on.

The Batarang whizzed from his hands, ricocheting from the skull of one thug to the next, one—two—three—four of them in front of him, and then the woman with the knives, knocking each one of them cold. Batman took a step forward as the Batarang swooped back behind him and knocked out that fifth thug who was sneaking up from the rear.

The Batarang whirred away from its final target, most of its momentum spent, and headed back toward Batman. A poodle jumped from a nearby doorway and caught the Batarang in its mouth. It leapt back to a woman in a ragged circus costume, and both of them took off down the alley.

Perhaps, Batman thought, he should take a minute to retrieve his property. He took a step toward the fleeing pair.

A man leapt into his path and proceeded to pull a sword

from his throat. Batman gave him a quick elbow to the ribs. The man doubled over, and Batman helpfully removed the sword for him.

He stepped over the sword swallower, and found himself facing a thin clown with three sticks of dynamite strapped to his chest along with a small clock face. It looked like some sort of homemade bomb.

"I'll blow up this whole—" the clown began.

Batman used the sword to cut the straps, then used the point to flip the bomb into his free hand. He rapped the clown's skull with the hilt. The clown sank to the ground.

Batman walked down the alley. He tossed the sword away.

He'd keep the bomb for a minute. You never knew when one would come in handy.

CHAPTER
Twenty-One

Catwoman ignored the gunfire, the sirens, even the screams. She didn't have time for that kind of destruction at the moment. She was looking forward to a little destruction of her own.

She walked up to the front door of Shreck's, the department store of her dreams. Or was that her nightmares? She was sure somebody was going to have nightmares before this night was done.

There was that cute Shreck logo of the kitten, etched onto the glass of the door.

How appropriate for Catwoman.

She punched it out with her claws.

That was even more appropriate, after all. This particular kitten had grown.

She reached within the broken glass and opened the door from within. The entire department store was hers. And she anticipated taking payment from it for everything that Max Shreck had done.

She held out her claws, ripping the silk blouses and designer originals from a whole row of mannequins. It wasn't enough. What she needed was music! There was a stereo on the floor here, used to urge the shoppers to get into the Christmas spirit. She quickly flipped through the tapes, discarding anything that had to do with Frosty the Snowman or little drummer boys. Ah, this was more like it! Some cool jazz. Just the sort of dance music for a cat on the prowl.

She turned up the music and looked to see what she could smash next. That glass jewelry case looked promising. She leapt on top of it, stomping her spiked heels down with all her weight.

"Oh, for me?" she called as the glass shattered beneath her, scattering gold and silver. "You shouldn't have!"

Maybe she'd come back and scarf up some of the better pieces before she left. But first she needed to do some more damage.

She stopped at the Sports Department. They had trampolines. She used to love trampolines! Heck, the destruction of the department store could wait. She wanted to take a bounce or two.

Whoops. She had company. Catwoman watched two security guards approach as she bounced up and down.

"Who is she?" one of them asked. A second later, he added, "What is she?"

The second one nodded, openmouthed. "I don't know whether to open fire, or fall in love."

"You poor guys," the Catwoman answered sadly, "always confusing your pistols with your privates."

Almost as if they had been waiting for their cue, both the guards drew their guns. Catwoman leapt from the trampoline, kicked the revolver from one hand, then whirled and slapped the gun away from the other guard. Neither one of them wanted to put up much of a fight. She cartwheeled over to the wall, and punched open a wall tile. Why, look what we have here. A propane tank! The way she knew her way around this place, she almost had to have help from the inside—like from a certain mousy administrative assistant?

She flicked out her claws and cut the propane line. Gas hissed out noisily.

"Don't hurt us!" one of the guards called defensively.

"Our take-home is under three hundred!" the other added.

"You're overpaid," Catwoman agreed. She stuck out a taloned thumb. "Hit the road."

The guards ran as Catwoman skipped over to the Automotive Department. All these aerosol cans would do the job quite nicely. Next stop would be "Today's Kitchen" and all those lovely microwaves. A few aerosol cans in a few microwaves, and those cheerful beeps as the microwaves were turned on, and hey—

Shreck's Department Store was going to have a party!

*   *   *

Batman staggered forward. Someone had hit him so hard in the back that he felt it even through his body armor. Batman spun around, and saw the Tatooed Strongman.

"Before I kill you, I let you hit me," the Tatooed Strongman said with a laugh. He flexed his tattoos. "Hit me. Come on, hit as hard as you can. I need a good laugh."

Batman pushed both his fists into the Tatooed Strongman's stomach. The Tatooed Strongman roared with laughter.

"You call that a—"

He stopped laughing when he saw that Batman hadn't used his hands to punch so much as to attach a bomb to the strongman's leopard skin. Before the Tatooed Strongman could react, Batman finally gave him a firm push, down a nearby open manhole. Amazing the way there were always open manholes around The Penguin's thugs.

The strongman's falling scream was cut short by an explosion. Smoke rose from the manhole as Batman turned away.

There, on the other side of the street, was The Penguin.

CHAPTER
Twenty-Two

The Penguin paused to shake the debris from his umbrella. My, things were certainly getting out of hand down here.

He looked up and saw Batman.

The Penguin tensed, ready to use one of his umbrella's special tricks. But instead of attacking, the man in the mask indicated the chaos around them.

"Admiring your handiwork?" Batman asked.

The Penguin shook his head vigorously. How wrong could a masked vigilante be? Hadn't Batman heard about his new image?

"Touring the riot scene," he explained soberly. "Gravely assessing the devastation. Upstanding mayor stuff."

Batman shook his head. "You're not the Mayor."

The Penguin shrugged. "Things change."

But why were they treating each other as adversaries? Two people of their particular sort—two outcasts from society—could do much better when they acted together. The Penguin stuck out one of his new-improved-image gloves to shake hands.

"Hey, good to meet you," he said in his best soon-to-be-mayor voice. "We'll be working hand in glove in Gotham's near and glorious future."

Batman didn't shake. Instead, he glanced around at all the lovely fires that had gotten started around the plaza.

"Once you were their freak," Batman remarked matter-of-factly. "Now these clowns work for you. Must feel pretty good."

Well, so much for the politician, The Penguin thought.

"Better than you know, Bat-boy," he replied.

"What are you really after?" Batman asked.

That sounded a little bit like a challenge. The Penguin smiled. "Ah, the direct approach. I admire that in a man with a mask." He poked his umbrella at Batman. "But you don't really think you'll win?"

The man with the mask smiled.

"Things change."

Oh, The Penguin thought, how droll. He wondered how droll Batman would be once Oswald Cobblepot put his master plan into effect. Now, how would he put that into words?

He stopped when he heard glass smash at the entryway to Shreck's Department Store. Both he and Batman turned to see a woman in black do a series of back flips across the plaza toward them. She performed a final somersault and came to her feet facing both of them.

Her costume was not only black, it was tight and shapely, and it made her look like a cat. This was one cat The Penguin would like to get to know better.

"Meow," she remarked.

And Shreck's Department Store exploded.

The Penguin looked out from under his umbrella. The flying glass seemed to have stopped. Much to his disappointment, the Catwoman seemed to have disappeared as well.

He glanced over at his other adversary.

"I saw her first," The Penguin remarked.

From the way Batman studied his surroundings, he did not appear amused. Apparently, the time for a polite chat was over. Perhaps it was time for The Penguin's exit.

"Gotta fly," he remarked as he hit the appropriate button on his umbrella. The steel rods that supported the fabric began to whirl about, first shredding the black cloth, then spinning free on their own, a compact rotor to send The Penguin into the air. In other words, an umbrella copter.

What a clever idea, huh, Batman? It was this sort of wit that would make The Penguin victorious. Where was Batman, anyway? He was running off someplace, not even waiting to say good-bye.

The Penguin grabbed his hat as he sailed away from danger and toward his destiny.

* * *

She had to be up here someplace.

Batman had used the winch and tackle in his utility belt to hoist him most of the way up here, but he'd have to negotiate the last couple of floors' worth of fire escape with his feet. He vaulted onto the roof of the building he had seen her climb only a minute ago. Now where would a Catwoman hide?

"Where's the fire?" came a voice behind him.

"Shreck's," Batman replied. He turned to see the Catwoman let herself down from a small rooftop shack. Her black costume had been torn in half a dozen places by the explosion, showing patches of pale flesh and a scratch or two.

"You—" he began.

She kicked him in the face. Batman staggered back with the blow, but recovered quickly, slamming her in the chin with one well-aimed blow. She fell backward into a whimpering ball.

"How could you?" she moaned from where she huddled on the rooftop. "I'm a woman—"

What did she mean? Had he hit her too hard? He was so used to fighting men.

"I'm sorry—" he began hesitantly. "I—"

Catwoman caught him in the chest with both her boots, sending him backward. He was headed over the ledge. He reached out his hands, looking for something to stop his fall.

Batman heard the crack of a whip, and felt a coil loop around one of his outstretched wrists. His hand was jerked roughly as he felt himself being pulled back toward the rooftop. This Catwoman had saved him with some sort of whip, and she lashed the other end of that whip to a weathervane, keeping Batman dangling over the edge and a killing drop.

"As I was saying," she remarked calmly. "I'm a woman and can't be taken for granted. Are you listening, you Batman, you?"

Was she kidding? Batman grimaced. "Hanging on every word?"

"Good joke," she replied. "Want to hear another one?"

Batman nodded cautiously. He didn't know how much encouragement he should give her.

"The world tells boys to conquer the world, and girls to wear clean panties," she explained. "A man dressed as a bat is a he-man, but a woman dressed as a cat is a she-devil." She ran her claws lightly over the whip that kept Batman tied to the roof. "I'm just living down to explanations. Life's a bitch—and now so am I."

She seemed done with talking for the moment. Batman quietly used his free arm to reach inside his utility belt to pull out a certain red and blue capsule.

"A he-man?" he replied with a dry laugh. "Sure. They shine that beacon in the sky, then wonder what hole I crawl out of."

"Wow," Catwoman remarked, "a real response and you're not even trying to get into my tights." She plucked the whip with one of her claws, nicking it ever so slightly. "But explain this to me—if you're so down on *them* out there, why bust your bat-buns to protect them?"

Batman shook his head. "I just can't sleep at night. Exploding department stores keep me up." He snapped the capsule in his hands, letting the red half flow into the blue. "One—"

"I can't sleep either, lately," Catwoman admitted. "A little link between us. But—bottom line, baby, you live to preserve the peace, and I'm dying to disturb it." She reached her claws forward to cut through the whip. "That could put a strain on our relationship."

"—four, five," Batman concluded. The tube in his hand had turned a bright purple and had started to bubble. He lobbed it at her arm as she cut away at the whip.

She screamed as the mixture exploded against her forearm. She lost her balance and fell past him, her claws catching on to a narrow ledge a few feet below. She scraped frantically at the concrete, trying to find someplace to dig in with her claws.

Batman freed his wrist from the remains of the whip and leapt down to her side. He grabbed her wrists and pulled her up, moving his hands beneath her armpits and then behind her back. The ledge was so narrow that he had to hold her quite close. It was almost as if they were embracing.

"Who are you?" she said as she gazed into his eyes. "Who's the man behind the Bat?" She smiled sadly. "Maybe he can help me find the woman behind the Cat." Her hand stroked his body armor. "That's not him. Ah—here you are."

Her hand stopped at that point just above the waist where the two main pieces of his armor joined. Without warning, she drove her talons through the fabric into his flesh.

Batman cried out in pain, pushing her away.

She fell.

"No," Batman whispered.

She hit the back of a passing truck filled with sand.

Catwoman jumped up and waved at the astonished Batman, who watched her from high above.

"Saved by the kitty litter," she remarked dryly. "Some date—"

She ripped her sleeve away to expose the nasty red welt on her forearm, looking at it more closely in the light of a passing street lamp.

"So it's not a corsage," she murmured. "But a burn lasts so much longer." So that was the Batman, she thought.

"Bastard," she added.

"Bitch," Batman muttered as he examined the wound, a set of four small punctures across his lower stomach. They felt much worse than they looked. Still, it was only when he had reached the safety of the Batcave that he felt he could sufficiently examine them.

He walked over to his communications console and flicked a switch, then pressed a button.

"Alfred," he called, "would you bring me some antiseptic ointment, please?"

"Coming," the concerned voice of the butler replied. "Are you in pain, sir?"

"Yes," Batman admitted, "a bit—" He flipped the switch back to break the connection.

"But I don't really mind," he added softly. He gingerly rubbed at his sore stomach, thinking about what had just happened, and with whom.

"Meow," he remarked.

CHAPTER
Twenty-Three

Her desk was so much cozier now. She had gotten rid of all those old, wimpy notes that Selina had written to herself and posted all over her computer, and replaced them with much more appropriate reminders: "Defy Authority." "Take No Prisoners." "Expose the Horror." Yes. She liked these much better.

A fly buzzed too close to her ear. She snatched it from the air and crushed it without looking up. It would be only one of the things she'd crush today.

But it was time for Max's coffee.

She grabbed the milk and made those final, all-important preparations.

She sauntered into Max's office. Chip was deep in conversation with his father; apparently an exploded department store was enough to get both their attentions.

"Morning, Max," she said to the old boss. "Bummer about the store. You covered?"

"I damn well better be!" the senior Shreck fumed. "In fact, I want you to phone those goniffs over at Gotham Insurance and tell them—"

"Actually," she replied casually, "I have to split. Take a 'personal day.' You don't mind? Max, you're tops!"

Max nodded. After her mysterious reappearance, he let her do just about anything. It was amazing what coming back from the dead could do for your career.

Max sipped his coffee. At last, the moment she'd been waiting for.

He made the strangest noise as he spit the live cockroach out of his mouth onto the table. And after that, he spent a good thirty seconds gagging.

Chip turned away from the table. The cockroach scurried off, leaving a coffee trail on Max's important papers.

"Those darned exterminators," she mentioned disparagingly. "They swore the machine was shipshape!"

She turned and sauntered out, listening to Max's continued gagging, sweet music to her sensitive ears. Yes, this day was starting out well enough. But it would get even better!

His chance was here at last. After that shameful night of crime on the streets of Gotham City, what could The Penguin—that is, Oswald Cobblepot—do but declare his candidacy for mayor? So they'd taken down the curtains, revealing his campaign headquarters for all to see. They'd invited the press, alerted the media, even come up with a couple of improved banners. OSWALD MEANS ORDER hung on the left side of the room. COBBLEPOT CAN CLEAN IT UP hung over the right.

So here he was, surrounded by the media and his hundred volunteers. What could The Penguin do to top that, except to say a few inspiring words?

"I may have saved the Mayor's baby," he said with a wave of his ever-present umbrella, "but I refuse to save a mayor who stood by, *helpless* as a baby, while Gotham was ravaged by a disease that turns Eagle Scouts into crazed clowns, and happy homemakers into Catwomen!" The Penguin wasn't exactly sure what this meant, but it sure sounded good.

His volunteers cheered. In the background, he could hear reporters calling in their stories: "Oswald Cobblepot, the mystery man-beast who's been romancing Gotham, today made a bid to run Gotham—"

Ah, it was music to his ears. What could be better?

A very shapely young volunteer stood in his path. "Mr. Cobblepot," she squealed as she looked adoringly down at him, "you're the coolest role model a young person could have."

Yes, he thought, it could get better, especially in the supply room, with the two of them alone.

"And you're the hottest young person a role model could have," he said aloud. He leaned forward and dropped his voice. "Here, wear a button."

It was, of course, his duty to pin that button personally

on her pert young breast. He wanted to see more of this volunteer—not to mention her pert young breasts—as soon as possible.

Ah, but there were still members of the press around. A politician had to be careful in these troubled times. He decided it might be best to go upstairs and cool off.

"I could really get into this mayor stuff," he murmured to himself. "It's not about power, it's about—reaching out to people. Touching people." He thought of his volunteer. "Groping people."

He climbed up to his other headquarters. The Organ Grinder was supervising the construction of those special weapons so necessary for their next assault. Everything looked to be in order here as well.

The thin Clown stuck his face up close to The Penguin.

"Hey, Penguin," he began, "there's a—"

The Penguin stomped down on the clown's foot.

"My name's not Penguin!" he barked. "It's Oswald Cobblepot." Especially, he thought, if that name attracted the babes. He almost felt like singing. Heck, why not? "I'll get a lot of tail on the campaign trail—"

"Oswald," the Knife Lady interjected, "there's someone here to see you." She jerked her head toward The Penguin's bed in the far corner of the loft. There, curled up on the mattress, with a pretty little kitty in her lap, was the woman of The Penguin's dreams—the Catwoman.

He chomped down hard on his cigarette holder. Be still, he told his heart—not to mention other parts of his anatomy. He'd show this beauty that fur and feathers could mix and mate.

The canary beside The Penguin's bed cried out in alarm, not at all pleased with the new visitors. But hey, what did canaries know? Maybe this Catwoman was dangerous, but it was The Penguin's kind of danger.

The Penguin stepped forward to greet her. "Just the pussy I've been looking for."

Catwoman sat up, moving her hands slowly up and down her upper arms. "Chilly in here."

She must be talking about those air conditioners on either side of his sleeping area, set up to re-create the temperature of his beloved Arctic World. One always tried to relive the comforts of one's childhood. But there was no reason this poor woman had to suffer for The Penguin's sake. At least not while they still had all their clothes on.

"I'll warm you!" he heartily volunteered.

"Down, Oswald," Catwoman warned.

The Penguin stopped. He didn't like the look of her claws.

"We need to talk," she continued. "You see, we have something in common."

"Sounds familiar," The Penguin agreed. He'd like to have a lot of things in common with this babe. "Appetite for destruction?" he guessed. He tugged on his suit coat. "Contempt for the czars of fashion? Wait—don't tell me—naked sexual charisma!"

"Batman," Catwoman replied simply. "The thorn in both our sides, the fly in our ointment."

"Ointment?" The Penguin leered. It sounded good to him. "Scented or unscented?"

Catwoman sighed and stood. "I'll come back later."

The Penguin gently pushed her back on the bed. Perhaps

he was coming on a bit too strong. Maybe they did need to talk for a minute or two before abandoning all their inhibitions and giving themselves up to overwhelming sexual passion.

"Are you, perchance, a registered voter?" he asked pleasantly. "I'm a mayoral prospect, you know."

She did not seem impressed. "I have but one pet cause today. Ban the Bat."

"Oh, him again," The Penguin replied dismissively. "what is it with you two? He's already history——" He raised his umbrella and pointed to the blueprints on the wall. "Check it out."

Catwoman walked over to the detailed diagrams of the Batmobile. It had taken Max a pretty penny to get them from the car's designer——or a disgruntled former employee of that designer. The Penguin let the businessman handle that sort of particular.

And speaking of particulars, they had every single part of the Batmobile labeled on these charts; and not just those parts the average citizen might see, but every nut and bolt that held that infernal machine together.

The Penguin chuckled at the very thought of their plans.

"We're going to disassemble his spiffy old Batmobile," he explained heartily, "then reassemble it as an H-bomb on wheels." He opened his umbrella as he made the sound of a muffled explosion——a visual aid for the death of Batman. "Yesterday's victor is tomorrow's vapor."

The Catwoman shook her head disapprovingly. "He'd have more power as a martyr. No, to destroy Batman, we must first turn him into what he hates most." She pointed at the Penguin, then herself. "Namely, us."

The Penguin frowned. This was more complicated than he thought. Was she talking about sullying the hero before they could off him?

"You mean, frame him?" he asked.

But Catwoman was no longer looking at him. She had noticed the huge pile of yellow legal pads on his bedside table, and had even picked up one to peruse the names he had written there.

"Hmm—not even in office yet," she mused, "and already an enemies list."

How dare she! The Penguin scurried over to his special project, thrusting his gloves forward to protect his list from unauthorized observation.

"These names are not for prying eyes!" He frowned up at this intruder. What did he know about this woman, anyway? "Hey, why should I trust some Catbroad? Maybe you're just a screwed-up sorority chick who's getting back at Daddy for not buying her that pony when she turned sweet sixteen—"

Or maybe, he thought but didn't say aloud, she was some sort of spy for the other side. Maybe even a spy for Batman.

She looked at him, nervous. He'd got under her fur with that last remark. Now what was he going to do with this Catwoman in his lair?

Before he could come to any conclusions, she reached into the birdcage and grabbed his pet canary. The Penguin bristled. If anything happened to his bird—

He grabbed one of the many umbrellas stacked by the side of the bed and pressed a button on the handle. A knife blade popped out of the top, a blade he used to pin Catwoman's little kitty cat against the bed.

He looked up at his adversary. The minute she swallowed the canary, her cat was history.

Catwoman spit Jerry from her mouth. The canary, somewhat damp but very much alive, flew up into the rafters.

Very well. A deal is a deal. The Penguin pulled his blade away from the kitty cat's throat. Catwoman protectively scooped up the cat in her arms. They stared at each other for a long moment.

What next? The Penguin thought. She freed one of her hands and leaned forward to gently stroke her claws against The Penguin's cheek. Petting from a Catwoman? It was one response he decided he could deal with.

"Look," she said, nodding at a scar below her wrist, "Batman napalmed my arm. He knocked me off a building just as I was starting to feel good about myself. I want to play an integral part in his degradation."

The Penguin regarded her for a moment. She certainly sounded sincere. And angry; that was important. The Penguin was big on anger.

"Well," he remarked slowly, "a plan is forming." He rubbed his chin with one of his gloves. "A vicious one, involving the loss of innocent life."

"I want in," Catwoman insisted. She shivered. "The thought of busting Batman makes me feel all—dirty. Maybe I'll give myself a bath right here."

She slowly ran her tongue along her upper arm. The Penguin licked his lips.

"You've got yourself a deal, puss," he replied huskily.

And with any luck, The Penguin had himself some action.

The Penguin was on TV. These days, it seemed like The Penguin was always on TV.

"I challenge the mayor," The Penguin declared with a melodramatic swoop of his umbrella, "to relight the Christmas tree in Gotham Plaza tomorrow night!"

Bruce Wayne looked up for an instant as Alfred placed his dinner before him.

The Penguin droned on through his media forum. "He must prove that under his administration, we can carry on our proud traditions without any fear. Not that I have any faith in the mayor," he squawked self-importantly, "but I pray, at least, the Batman will be there to preserve the peace."

"Sir," Alfred remarked, disturbing his concentration. "Shall we change the channel to a program with some dignity and class? *The Love Connection*, perhaps?"

Alfred was right. Bruce couldn't become obsessed with this Penguin's preening. But this crook had just offered a challenge to Batman, and Batman couldn't help but accept. Bruce wondered exactly what The Penguin planned to do at the tree lighting. Whatever it was, Batman had to be ready for it.

Maybe, he considered, there might be a way that Batman could be there without The Penguin's knowledge.

He looked one more time at The Penguin, talking away on the TV screen.

"Subtle," he remarked.

As a flying mallet, he thought to himself.

He reached for the remote, and turned The Penguin off.

A rehearsal, he thought, for the real thing, when Batman turned The Penguin off forever.

CHAPTER
Twenty-Four

It was almost Christmastime.

Remarkably, they had managed to reopen some of the stores on the plaza, making quick repairs to the devastation of a couple days ago. When he had left here that night, Bruce would have thought this kind of recovery was impossible. Still, he guessed that nothing was stronger than the lure of Christmas cash.

Bruce saw a boy, walking between his mother and father, as all three headed for the restored window of the toy store. The boy seemed so happy. And why shouldn't he be? He had his parents. They all had each other at Christmastime.

Bruce had to turn away.

His mother screamed. His father tried to stop them. He heard the gunshots.

Bruce opened his eyes. Christmas.

Bruce could not think of a more depressing time of year.

When he turned, he saw a woman looking at a store window; a woman whom he recognized. And a woman he would very much like to get to know better. He walked her way. Maybe he could cheer up after all.

"Why are you doing this?" she said to her reflection. She didn't appear to be happy herself. Maybe there was some way, Bruce thought, that he could cheer the both of them up.

He tapped her on the shoulder.

She jumped.

"Selina," he said softly as she turned to stare at him. "Hi. Didn't mean to—"

She placed one delicate hand on her heaving chest. Once she recognized Bruce, she seemed relieved to see him. Could that be a good sign?

"Scare me?" she replied. "No, actually, I was just scaring myself."

"I don't see how," Bruce replied, doing his best to lighten the conversation. "Anyway, it's a treat to find you out in the world, away from Ebenezer Shreck."

"Treat to be here," she valiantly replied. She sighed as if she could not possibly mean it. She took a step away from the window.

"What's the story?" Bruce asked as he fell into step beside her. "Holiday blues?"

But Selina pointed at the Plaza Newsstand as they

walked on past, full of newspapers with blazing banner headlines about the night before:

BATMAN BLOWS IT!
IT'S A CAT-ASTROPHE
MEE-OUCH!

"The news these days," she explained, "weird. People looking to superheroes for their peace of mind, and blaming their problems on supervillains—instead of themselves, or their spouses at least."

Yes, Bruce had to admit, those kind of headlines annoyed him, too. What kind of reflection were they on the realities of last night's battle?

"And it's not even accurate," he complained. "I mean, 'Batman Blows It'? The guy probably prevented millions in property damage!"

Selina nodded in agreement. "I heard on TV—'Catwoman is thought to weigh one hundred and forty pounds!' How do these hacks *sleep* at night?"

Their further progress appeared to be blocked by the preparations for the upcoming ceremony. Police were putting up cordons to keep the public away from a large portion of the square in front of the tree. A pair of workmen hoisted a new banner above the plaza that announced the exact timing of the event:

THE RELIGHTING OF THE TREE
TONIGHT AT SEVEN

Selina looked up at the banner, even more unhappy than before. "You're not coming to that, are you? The 'Relighting of the Tree' thing?"

"I wouldn't be caught dead," Bruce agreed. "No, it's probably how I would be caught." He sighed exasperatedly. "The mayor stupidly took Cobblepot's bait—"

"—and it's going to be a hot time on the cold town tonight," Selina said with a little laugh.

Bruce looked over at her. This was the first time he'd heard her voice rise out of the doldrums.

"You almost sound enthusiastic," he mentioned.

She looked back at Bruce and shrugged.

"Oh, no, I detest violence but—" She paused, as if it was difficult for her to put her exact feelings into words. "Christmas complacency can be a downer, too."

It was Bruce's turn to chuckle. "You've got a dark side, Selina. Hmm?"

She looked at him with those piercing blue eyes. "No darker than yours, Bruce."

He certainly couldn't deny that.

"Well, I'm—braver at night," he admitted, "if that's what you mean."

"Yeah?" She looked at him with a smile. "Me, too."

They started to walk alongside the yellow police line, passing the stage where the Ice Princess once again rehearsed for the important job of pressing the button that would light the tree.

He turned back to Selina, his voice soft as he suggested, "Maybe we'll watch it on TV."

" 'We'?" Now Selina turned to look at him. She actually smiled. "You and—"

"Me," he finished for her, realizing only then that he had invited this beautiful woman into his life. Wait a moment; there was something wrong with what he had just said.

"No," he corrected himself, "that would make it me and me." He paused. Hadn't they had this conversation before? "Is that what I said?"

Selina laughed. "Yes and no," she replied.

They turned toward the curb. There was his Rolls-Royce, pulling up to the curb to whisk them away. Bruce was sometimes amazed that Alfred could be so good at timing this sort of thing.

Maybe, Bruce thought, Batman could miss tonight's festivities after all.

He took Selina's hand. She didn't object. Together, they walked toward the waiting car.

This evening would be everything he'd planned!

The Penguin waddled into the tent that held the controls for tonight's celebration, as well as the dressing room of that well-built Ice Princess. He could hear her talking to herself as he approached.

"The tree lights up, I press the button," she mused. "No, wait, I press the button first and the tree—"

"Who are you?" she demanded as he marched into her dressing room.

"Talent scout," The Penguin reassured her.

Her frigid demeanor disappeared behind the most charming of smiles. Hey! A talent scout? He was her kind of people. "Come in!" she insisted. "You know, I don't just light trees. I studied the Method. Well, it was by mail, but—"

She stopped when she saw that The Penguin was accompanied by a poodle with an odd-looking box in his mouth.

Now, The Penguin just had to use that little box. Nice doggie. The poodle growled. He had to yank it free.

"What is that?" she asked prettily. "A camera or something?"

The Penguin nodded most agreeably. No need for her to know it was the Batarang that they'd stolen from Batman. She'd find out about that soon enough.

He jauntily punched a series of buttons. "Say 'Cheese,' " he remarked.

The wings sprouted out of the Batarang's sides.

She never knew what hit her.

CHAPTER
Twenty-Five

Chestnuts roasting on an open fire, Jack Frost nipping at your nose—

Selina Kyle—and tonight, she did feel like Selina should have always felt—looked up from where she sat next to Mr. Bruce Wayne on what might be the world's most comfortable couch. They were sitting very close together. Not only was there romantic music on the CD player, but the couch faced a roaring fire, and Alfred the butler—an actual butler!—had reappeared, silently—she wondered how butlers did that—to refill their eggnogs. Wow. Mr. Bruce Wayne, handsome, clever, and interested in her besides! Why couldn't she have met him long ago—say, before Catwoman entered the picture?

She smiled at Alfred. He smiled back and disappeared just as silently as he had arrived.

She turned back to Bruce. "I'm sure he's wonderful company and all, but—doesn't the gold-plated bachelor bit get a little—stale?"

Bruce smiled at that—imagine, a man who smiled at her attempts at humor—and replied, "Somewhat like the lonely-secretary syndrome, I'd suppose."

Secretary?

"Executive assistant," was her automatic response. But who was she kidding, especially working for somebody like Max Shreck?

"Secretary," she admitted.

But she had other, more important questions to ask.

"Girlfriend?" was first among them.

Bruce looked straight into her eyes. "As in 'serious'? Had one. Didn't work." He took a drink of eggnog.

"What went wrong?" she asked. "Hang on, I think I know." After all, what always went wrong with all of her relationships? "You kept things from her."

But Bruce shook his head.

"Nope, I told her everything."

Oh, Selina thought, now this was far more interesting.

"And the truth frightened her?" she asked.

Bruce put his eggnog down on the table in front of them and turned all his attention to her. My, she thought, a girl could get used to this.

"Well—" he began hesitantly, "how can I put this. There were two truths"—he opened his two hands, as if he could hold one of those truths in each of them—"and she had trouble reconciling them." He sighed as his hands came together. "Because I had trouble reconciling them." He sighed again. "So Vicki said."

"Vicki?" She couldn't help herself. She giggled. Vicki. What a perfect name for the girlfriend of a millionaire bachelor playboy.

"Ice skater or stewardess?" she guessed.

"Photojournalist," Bruce replied.

"Sure," Selina replied. Just like she was an executive assistant.

She looked at Bruce and they both started to laugh.

"Well?" Selina insisted, trying again to be serious. "Was 'Vicki' right? About your difficulty with duality?"

Bruce hesitated again. He was so sincere when he hesitated. "If I said yes, then you might think me a Norman Bates, or a Ted Bundy type"—he paused, and hesitantly leaned forward—"and then you might not let me kiss you."

It was about time. She didn't wait for him to finish leaning. She decided to move forward and kiss him instead.

The kiss lasted for a while. Who needed words, when he had this set of lips? Explanations came and went, but a good kiss was forever.

They finally had to come up for air. She looked at him very seriously. A kiss like that deserved an answer.

"It's the so-called normal guys who always let you down," she said. "Sickos never scared me. At least they're committed."

He put his arms around her then.

"Ah," Bruce whispered. "Then you've come to the right lonely mansion."

They kissed again, and this one promised much more to come. She found her fingers playing with the buttons on his shirt, and then unbuttoning them, one after another. She started from the top, and worked her way down.

His hand covered hers on the third button. He pushed her gently away. Was she going too fast? This sort of thing was always difficult to time. If only he wasn't such a good kisser.

Then his hand moved over and started to play with her buttons? Uh-oh. The male wanted to run the show? Well, maybe Selina would allow it—this time.

But wait. If he took off her blouse how would she explain the burn on her arm? Maybe she had better wait herself.

Reluctantly, she pushed his exploring hand away.

Bruce seemed every bit as embarrassed as she did.

"I, uh," he sputtered, "I never fool around on the first date."

His hand brushed against his stomach, as if checking on something beneath the shirt.

At least he was being chivalrous enough to give her an out. "Nor I, on the second," she agreed. Still, she didn't know how long she could hold out around somebody like him. How long would it take for that sort of burn to heal?

Bruce looked at her. "What are you doing three dates from now?"

Selina stood abruptly, crossing the room to the TV set. Don't tempt me, she thought. Please tempt me.

"Weren't we going to watch the relighting of the tree?" she said instead. She pushed the on button on the TV.

Instead of the ceremonies, the TV screen was filled with scenes of an all-too-familiar chaos in Gotham Plaza.

"We repeat," an announcer said from where he stood in the midst of a surging and screaming crowd, "the Ice Princess has been kidnapped! And it only gets worse— Commissioner Gordon—"

The scene shifted to the police commissioner, looking pale and visibly shaken, as he stood before a tent elsewhere in Gotham Plaza.

The announcer continued, "Can you confirm the reports we're hearing of Batman's suspected involvement in the abduction?"

"The evidence is purely circumstantial," Gordon replied with a frown. "We found this, stained with blood, in the missing girl's dressing room." He held up some kind of a box with wings. It sure looked like it belonged to Batman.

She looked back at Bruce. The Penguin had set his plans in motion. And Catwoman had promised to be there. Instead, she was on the other side of town, and had almost let a man take control. That's what she got for letting Selina do the thinking. But was there any way The Penguin would trust Catwoman now?

Bruce looked upset as well. Probably had something to do with all this violence in the city. She wished her problems were that simple!

He stood, and smiled almost apologetically.

"Selina," he said quickly, "I'm just going to check on those chestnuts Alfred was roasting."

There was no reason to be apologetic about that, was there? If anyone should be apologetic around here, it should be her, because she had to get out of here.

Catwoman had an appointment.

CHAPTER
Twenty-Six

Alfred strode across the foyer, a bowl of roasted chestnuts in his hands. He heard Master Wayne's footsteps before he saw him, allowing him to neatly sidestep his employer and thus avoid collision.

"Sorry, Alfred," Mr. Wayne gulped, trying hard to regain his breath. "I have to get to the Plaza. You heard The Penguin, he was practically begging me to show."

Alfred did find this most recent statement disappointing. "Which is why I hoped you'd snub him," he remarked calmly.

Bruce took a step away, already heading toward the entrance to his secret cave. "I'm afraid I can't. There's been a kidnapping. Tell Selina—that is, Ms. Kyle—that some business came up . . ." He hesitated, shaking his head. "No, tell her that some major deal fell through, she'll feel sorry—" More head shakes as he looked up toward heaven, for inspiration perhaps, then down toward the Batcave. "—No, no, here's what to do, just tell her— let her know that—not in a dumb 'Be my girlfriend way,' but—"

Alfred already knew precisely what to say.

"I will relay the message," he reassured his employer.

"All right," Bruce replied, "thanks."

He ran down the hallway.

Alfred turned back toward the den to fulfill his duty.

And almost ran into Ms. Selina Kyle as she rushed into the foyer.

"Alfred!" she said brightly. "Hi! I—"

The butler decided he should dispense with Mr. Wayne's apologies immediately.

"Ms. Kyle," he began evenly. "Mr. Wayne has asked me to let you know that—"

"Mr. Wayne," Selina replied, as if she still wasn't quite used to the name. "Bruce." She took a deep breath. "Yes—would you tell him for me that I've been going through a lot of changes and—" She shook her head. "No, don't say that." She frowned and then continued. "Just . . . this is not a rejection, my abruptly leaving. It's . . . in fact, tell him that he makes me feel the way I hope I really am—*no*."

She laughed helplessly, throwing up her hands. "If you can whip up a sonnet, something—" She shrugged and laughed. "A dirty limerick?"

Alfred nodded reassuringly. "One has just sprung to mind."

Ms. Kyle laughed again and opened the front door.

Yes, Alfred thought, he liked this young woman. In fact, it appeared that she and Master Bruce were virtually made for each other.

He would have to frame the precise words to relate to his employer.

A butler's work was never done.

It was too bad, really. They had come so close.

But Bruce didn't want to have to explain those scars on his stomach. Not yet. Batman had gotten in the way of Bruce Wayne's last relationship. And he supposed he would eventually have to let his alter ego into this relationship as well, but somehow he wanted a little romance before the complications set in.

Bruce quickly donned the suit.

And Batman jumped into the Batmobile and headed for downtown Gotham City.

She was so glad she had decided to drive herself to Wayne Manor.

When Bruce had ushered her into the car, he had asked if she wanted to come up to the house now, or wait until the evening. She had opted for the evening, and directions to the mansion, even though Bruce had volunteered Alfred's chauffeuring services.

A woman, after all, needed her independence.

Now, though, she needed to be in Gotham Plaza. She dug down under the old magazines and diet cola cans to pull out her Catwoman costume.

Romance was nice, but she craved action.

* * *

The Batman guided the Batmobile into a deserted alley immediately behind the plaza.

At first glance it appeared that the police had managed to restore some order to the proceedings. Still, he needed to be here. He was sure the capture of the Ice Princess wasn't The Penguin's only plan, but part of some larger picture. And Batman wanted to be there when The Penguin pulled something new from his soiled sleeve.

He jumped from the car, pausing only long enough to activate the Batmobile's security shields. Then he headed swiftly and silently toward the plaza, his dark costume blending with the shadows.

Fools! Let them try to establish order.

The only orders around here would come from The Penguin.

Still, they tried to set the klieg lights working, swinging back and forth as if nothing were wrong. And there was the mayor—soon to be the ex-mayor—pitifully attempting to restore order.

"People!" he yelled into his microphone. "Fellow citizens. There's no need for panic. This can still be a party that Gotham will remember for—"

Whatever he wanted to say next was lost under a shriek of feedback. Now how could something like that happen? Surely, it had nothing to do with The Penguin twisting the knobs on the controls to the speaker system?

And while The Penguin was busy helping the mayor, his helpers were busy making adjustments of their own.

Even from his hiding place within the tent, he could tell what they were doing.

The Poodle Lady led the way, her mangy dog at her side. And following her were all their circus chums. But none of them came to the party empty-handed, for each of them carried a toolbox.

And the name of the party was the Batmobile.

One of the Red Triangle Circus Gang climbed atop the security shield, and with the aid of a primitive but still quite effective hand-held laser, disabled the whole system. Whoosh, and the shield was gone. The rest of the gang rushed up at that, each member equipped with a very special helmet containing a very detailed drawing that outlined their own very specific task.

And once all those tasks were put together, the Red Triangle Circus Gang would take the Batmobile apart.

[illegible] that they were [illegible].

The people [illegible] the [illegible] side. [illegible] were all [illegible] ones of [illegible] another.

And the name of the game was [illegible].

[illegible]

And in all those cases [illegible] would help the Batman [illegible]

CHAPTER
Twenty-Seven

B atman watched the events in Gotham Plaza from the shadows.

The mayor was valiantly attempting to calm the crowd, but half his speech was lost in feedback.

"—incess will be safely—" managed to get through the noise. "—atman will be brought in for question—"

But Batman had no more time for the mayor's words, for he saw a light on in a window across from him, and in that window was the bound and gagged Ice Princess.

There was no time for explanations to the mayor. Not yet. He shot out a grapple and line to the ledge above. In a short time, his actions would speak far louder than his words.

* * *

The Penguin played the control knobs like they were a grand piano. Let in a few words here, a few words there, just enough to give the mayor hope he could be heard while totally confusing his audience.

His minions had by now totally dismantled the Batmobile. Ah, but that was only the beginning of the fun. For now they added a clamp here, twisted a wire there, so that the controls no longer acted in quite the way they did before. And the pièce de résistance? Why, that special antenna they installed on the underside of the car, so that the Batmobile could be totally controlled by an outside signal—a signal managed by someone who was very good at twisting knobs.

Batman crashed through the window, into the room that held the Ice Princess. The place was bare except for the woman and the chair that they had tied her to. He quickly crossed the room and pulled the gag from her mouth. She started to thank him as he examined the ropes that held her.

"We've got to hurry," he explained. "I was set up to look like I did this."

"No sweat," the Ice Princess replied brightly. "I'll just tell the police I was kidnapped by an ugly birdman with fish breath."

Another woman's voice cut in: "Did someone say 'fish'?"

Catwoman dropped down from somewhere overhead.

"Yummy," she remarked. "I haven't been fed all day."

She leapt forward, kicking out at Batman. He stepped

aside, grabbing her heel and allowing the momentum to flip her all the way over.

"Eat floor," he replied. "It's high fiber."

But Catwoman sprang up easily. "Hey, stud," she pouted. "I thought we had something together."

"We do," Batman replied as he sprang forward, knocking his head against hers. Of course, his head was reinforced with body armor.

She reeled but it was only an instant before she shook it off. He found her more impressive with every encounter. She back-flipped away from him, straight for the Ice Princess. A single swipe of her talons cut the ropes that held the other woman.

"Gotta go," Catwoman called. "Girl talk! Guys keep out!" She threw the chair at Batman as she pulled the squealing princess through a doorway. The door slammed shut behind them.

Batman swatted the chair out of the way and crossed the room in three quick strides. The door was locked, deadbolted.

He took a step back, then kicked it open with his boot.

They weren't in the hallway.

He heard the princess scream. The sound came from an open window on the far side of the hall. Catwoman had taken the princess up the fire escape.

Batman took the steps up as fast as he could. He saw the two women disappear before he had climbed halfway to the roof.

He couldn't stop now. He tried to control his breathing as he took the metal stairs two and three at a time. He had to have enough left to fight whatever he found on the roof.

It was quiet above. No more sounds of struggle. Batman leapt onto the rooftop, ready to dodge or to fight.

Catwoman was nowhere to be seen. Instead, the Ice Princess shivered alone in her skimpy costume at the far edge of the roof.

"She let me go," the princess explained. "I think because I reasoned with her, girl to girl."

This was too easy. Batman was afraid this wasn't over. He took his first tentative steps toward the princess. "Okay," he said levelly, "just slowly move toward me, away from the edge."

The Ice Princess tried to smile. She took her first tentative step forward.

"Look out!" The Penguin stepped out from behind an old chimney. "Lawn dart!"

He threw an umbrella straight at the Ice Princess. Its sharp point embedded itself in the rooftop, inches away from the princess's toes. She took a step away.

"No," Batman called. "Don't panic!"

The umbrella dropped open, releasing a cloud of tiny flying bats. The Ice Princess screamed, trying somehow to get away from the flock of flying mammals.

Batman ran toward her. But she was too close to the edge. The klieg light shone up from down below, highlighting her silhouette as she lost her balance on the building's edge.

He leapt out to grab her. But she was gone. She fell into the klieg light's beam, down to her death.

CHAPTER
Twenty-Eight

Commissioner Gordon despaired at returning order to the streets.

He had a hundred uniformed policemen stationed around the plaza, and twenty more watched the scene from the upper stories of surrounding buildings. He knew The Penguin or some of his gang were around here somewhere. And as soon as they showed themselves, Gordon swore that this time the police would be ready for them.

A voice barked static on his remote walkie-talkie.

"Gordon here," he replied as he pressed the talk button. The Sergeant filled him in from Precinct 12. Someone had tipped off the department; the Ice Princess was being held on the top of a building on the far side of the plaza.

Gordon issued instructions for a number of units to meet

him at the scene as he hurried through the crowd. Maybe this was the break he had been hoping for.

Somebody shouted and pointed toward the roofs above. There, silhouetted in the sweeping klieg light, was Batman, racing across the rooftop with arms outstretched. A second light picked up the form of the missing Ice Princess, on the very edge of the building. The lights swept away for an instant, then back again, as Batman reached the young woman, and the young woman fell from the rooftop!

"Batman?" someone yelled in the crowd. "Batman pushed the princess!"

The commissioner frowned. The way the sweeping lights had left the scene, there was no way to tell exactly what had happened. It was much more likely that Batman was trying to save her. But there was no way you could tell that to an angry crowd.

He called to the cops around him. He had to get up on that rooftop, and he needed reinforcements.

The Penguin's plans were perfect.

The Ice Princess fell, screaming. No one in the crowd made a sound as she plummeted toward the platform. She hit with a sickening crunch.

And The Penguin heard new sounds coming from the Christmas tree.

The button that controlled the lighting of the tree was on the platform. Her body must have hit it at the end of her fall.

So she had been able to do her job after all. Too bad it was the last job she would ever do.

And when her dying body hit the button, did it simply

light the tree? Oh, no, that would have been much too simple. Instead of lights, The Penguin had filled the tree with cages full of bats, all released at the press of that button. Very suggestive, if The Penguin did say so himself. The crowd screamed and panicked as the bats swooped among them.

"Rats with wings," The Penguin remarked chipperly, "do your things—"

He looked across the roof. Oh, yes, Batman was still here. Well, that would be taken care of shortly.

Batman headed for him in a way that suggested he intended to do great bodily harm.

Penguin heard the commotion on the stairs. He stepped back so he would be behind the fire door when the police arrived.

They took the elevators to the top floor, then headed up the stairs to the roof. There were a dozen cops in riot gear in front of Gordon, maybe two dozen more behind him. They should be able to handle anything.

The men in front of him burst through the door above and quickly fanned out, guns at the ready. Gordon followed as quickly as his weight and age would allow.

He reached the roof to see all guns pointed at the Batman, outlined by the klieg lights at the edge of the roof.

"Wait!" Batman called.

"Hold your fire!" Gordon began.

But his words were lost under gunfire as a hail of bullets pushed Batman off the edge of the roof.

light the [illegible]. [illegible] would have [illegible] [illegible]. Instead, [illegible]. The [illegible] had [illegible] [illegible]. They were [illegible]. The [illegible] and [illegible] as the [illegible] among them.

"[illegible]," The [illegible] on your [illegible]—"

He looked [illegible]. [illegible] was still here. Well, that would be [illegible] care of [illegible].

[illegible] in a way that [illegible] to [illegible] totally [illegible].

[illegible] the [illegible] on the stairs. [illegible] the door [illegible] the [illegible] arrived.

[illegible]

[illegible]

[illegible]

CHAPTER
Twenty-Nine

H is body armor had saved him. That, and the fact that he had only fallen a short distance, to a penthouse terrace maybe a dozen feet below.

He tried to stand, and found himself pushed back to the ground by a high-heeled boot.

Catwoman stood above him. Boot still on his chest, she smiled down at him.

"You're catnip to a girl like me," she purred. "Handsome, dazed, and to die for."

She stepped back and leaned down, as if she were going to kiss him. She licked him instead, cat style, across the lips. Batman looked up above her head and realized she was holding a sprig of mistletoe.

"A kiss under the mistletoe?" he managed, still trying

to regain his breath. "Mistletoe can be deadly, if you eat it—"

Catwoman smiled, her face still only a few inches away. "But a kiss can be even deadlier, if you mean it."

She reached down to his utility belt, and unfastened it with a single flick of her claws. She pulled it from his waist and tossed it off the side of the roof.

"You're the second man who killed me this week," she remarked sadly. "But, hey, no prob. I've got seven lives left."

Killed her? He realized she must mean her own fall from that other roof. Maybe now he could explain.

"I tried to grab you—save you—"

She looked meaningfully toward the edge of the roof. "Seems like every woman you try to save winds up dead"—she turned back to Batman—"or deeply resentful."

She grabbed his armor with her claws and yanked him to his feet.

"Maybe," she suggested, "it's time to retire." She swiped toward his mask with her claws.

It was time to get out of here. Batman jumped backward, away from her and off the roof. This time, though, he was ready for the fall.

He pressed a small button at his waist, and twin wings sprouted from either side of his armor, turning him into a glider that would gently sail down to the ground.

He swooped down, surrounded by the rising bats from the Christmas tree below. That must be another of The Penguin's special touches. He'd have to thank the bird man personally, as soon as he'd had a chance to recover.

He banked over the crowd, heading for the alley and the Batmobile. He was coming in very fast. He'd have to skirt over the top of the crowd, then try to hit the pavement running. With luck, he could fold in the wings and somersault to a stop.

The alley wasn't large enough for the wings. He tried to pull them close as he touched down, but the wings were too awkward to maneuver in this narrow space. He lost his footing, and went from a run to a stumble. The left wing shattered against a brick wall as he collapsed forward, skidding on the pavement.

Batman groaned. He had hit the ground hard. The ground spun around before him. But he had to get up. Safety was only a few feet away.

He had to get to the Batmobile.

The Catwoman and The Penguin sat on the edge of the terrace, watching the Batman's wings collapse in the alley.

My, she thought, that did look painful. All in all, a very satisfying fall for the Batman.

And The Penguin had brought champagne.

He handed over a glass.

She looked back at The Penguin. How could he be so happy? Well, of course, they had totally framed and humiliated the Batman. But someone had gotten killed in the process.

"You said you were going to *scare* the Ice Princess!" she said with a frown.

"And I kept my word!" The Penguin replied with continued joviality. "The lady looked terrified."

Catwoman frowned down at the glass of champagne.

She was beginning to think The Penguin wasn't her kind of person.

He reached within one of the many pockets of his soiled coat, and pulled forth what must once have been a box from Tiffany's. It was now rather the worse for the wear, both worn and stained, as if it had spent a long time with The Penguin down in the sewers.

He opened the box, revealing a golden ring that was so overdone with gaudy, amazingly, even horrifying gems that it was hideous; almost like someone had lost their lunch in a jewelry store. She looked back at The Penguin. What was he trying to prove?

"So what are we waiting for?" he urged. "Let's consummate our fiendish union!"

Union? She frowned.

"Oh, please," she said with a shudder. "I wouldn't touch you to scratch you!"

That apparently was the wrong answer. The Penguin began to quake with rage.

"I oughta have you spayed!" he shouted. "You sent out all the signals!"

Catwoman paused to think about that.

"Did I?" she asked. And silently answered, maybe she did. "Only because my mom trained me to, with a man—" Oh yeah. She remembered her mom's warnings. Heaven forfend Selina should be an Old Maid! "—any man," she added, "—all men—"

This Cat outfit had brought it out even more. Why couldn't she look at what she was doing? "Corn dog!" she muttered, hitting herself on the side of the head for good measure.

But why was she blaming herself again? She had promised that once she had donned the Catwoman outfit, she would place the blame where it belonged—on men! She turned to The Penguin with a new resolve.

"Me, domesticated?" she asked angrily. "By you? I doubt it! You repulsive, awful—" She hesitated for an instant, looking for some sufficiently insulting way to end the remark, but there really was only one way to complete the sentence. "—Penguin!"

The Penguin hugged his umbrella close, mortally offended. "The name is Oswald Cobblepot."

He flung the umbrella at her. She dodged the shaft, but the handle snaked around her neck, forming a noose as the ribs of the umbrella spun above her, creating a rotor that lifted her from the roof. She couldn't breathe.

The Penguin waved sadly as the umbrella copter lifted her from the ground.

"And the wedding's been called *off*."

He was going to hang her with his umbrella!

CHAPTER
Thirty

S he saw The Penguin turn moodily away as the umbrella whirled her away from the rooftop and out over Gotham City.

But she would strangle. There had to be some way to loosen this noose. She reached up with her claws, striking at the rope that stretched across the back of her neck.

She sliced through it. She could breathe.

But she was no longer being held aloft by the umbrella, which went spinning ever higher as she fell.

She saw lights immediately below. A glass enclosure on another roof. A penthouse maybe.

She crashed through the roof.

She opened her eyes. She had landed in dirt, surrounded by flowers. This wasn't just a penthouse, it was a greenhouse.

So Catwoman survived. But was she happy?

She wailed loud enough to break the rest of the glass.

Another life down the tubes.

There were banners and posters all over the place—windows, telephone poles, even the campaign bus—and all saying, in a dozen different ways, to vote Cobblepot for Mayor.

The Penguin loved those slogans. Max's boys were so good at those sort of things.

His supporters clustered around him, cheering. So why couldn't he shake this gloom? Maybe it had something to do with killing not one babe, but two! It seemed like such a waste of good womanflesh—especially before he and those babes could become more personally acquainted. He pulled a handful of campaign buttons out of one of his many pockets, and started to pin them on the chests of his supporters—his female supporters—his well-endowed female supporters. Hey, he started to feel better already. What was a dead babe or two, when there were all these other babes to go around?

Still, he had other fish to fry at the moment. After waving a fond adieu, especially to a couple of blondes, he jumped aboard his bus and hurried back to his specially designed miniature Batmobile, complete with switches, meters, dials, knobs, levers, buttons, and a mini-steering wheel. What made this even more special, of course, was that every single button, lever and knob on this board controlled some function of the real Batmobile.

Hey. The Penguin cackled. This could cheer him up even more.

His body had taken too much abuse; too many punches and kicks and bullets, compounded by his crash into the alley. His body armor had absorbed some of the shock. But his body had received the rest of it.

Somehow, Batman got to his feet. Somehow, he made it to the Batmobile. He pressed a button beneath his glove and switched off the security system.

And not a moment too soon, he thought, as he heard angry voices behind him. He could make out enough of their shouts as he popped open the door to the Batmobile to figure out the source of their anger. They wanted him, and not necessarily alive. They thought he had murdered the Ice Princess. In their minds, he was already tried, convicted, and ready for execution. Now that they'd found him, they weren't going to let him get away; a whole mob of self-appointed vigilantes.

Vigilantes. It had a familiar ring to it. What made them so different from Batman?

Only perhaps that he had the money for the proper training, and the state-of-the-art equipment. And maybe, just maybe, he had his anger under a little more control.

The voices were getting closer. The leading edge of the crowd was only a few yards away.

Now wasn't the time to think about this. Now it was time to get out of here.

He jumped into the driver's seat and slammed the door shut above him. The mob couldn't reach him now. He exhaled, giving himself a moment's peace before he took the Batmobile home.

The doors locked. The control panel flashed on. The engine roared to life.

Batman stared at the controls. He hadn't touched anything.

The small TV monitor by the side of the wheel blipped on. But instead of Alfred's face, Batman saw the gloating features of The Penguin.

"Don't adjust your set," the villain remarked pleasantly. "Welcome to the Oswald Cobblepot School of Driving. Gentlemen, start your screaming—"

The Batmobile slammed forward as if Batman had floored the accelerator. Batman's pursuers jumped wildly for cover as the car careened forward and turned, tires squealing, onto the street.

The Penguin had it all!

He had two screens in front of him. One showed him Batman's face. Very tense. Definite Type A personality. If Batman wasn't careful, he'd get an ulcer. That is, if he lived long enough. Which he wouldn't.

The second screen showed a driver's-eye view of where the Batmobile was going. Very important, since The Penguin was doing the steering. And no doubt he would steer the Batmobile straight into an accident. But it had to be a spectacular accident. And the Batmobile should run over as many innocent bystanders as possible before it happened.

After all, why only sully a hero's reputation when, with just a little more effort, you could destroy it completely?

"Maybe this would be a bad time to mention it," The Penguin said to his own personal video camera, the one whose signal was being piped to the Batmobile, "but my license has expired."

He turned the Batmobile toward the crowd-filled plaza, and once again pressed his own personal accelerator.

"Of course," The Penguin added with a cackle, "so have you."

Afterward, why [illegible] should [illegible] when [illegible] a telepathic effect, we could [illegible] a temporary [illegible]

"Maybe this would [illegible]" The Penguin [illegible]

[illegible]

[illegible] the Demon [illegible]

[illegible]

"[illegible]," the Penguin added with a [illegible] "[illegible] hate you."

CHAPTER
Thirty-One

B atman was in the middle of a nightmare.

First, his car had been taken out of his control. Batman punched out the instrument panel in front of him. It looked like half the system had been rewired.

How had they managed this? He had only left the Batmobile alone for a few minutes. The time and expertise to accomplish this sort of thing was staggering. They had not only rigged the Batmobile, they had also foiled those warning systems he had built in to tell him of just this sort of tampering.

And once the car was under another's control, it was being driven at top speed directly toward the Christmas crowds. Apparently, The Penguin wouldn't be satisfied with only the Batman's death. He wanted innocent bystanders to die as well.

Batman had underestimated his opponent. And he would pay for it, unless he could figure out some way to retake control.

Batman ripped out a handful of the new wiring, then a second. The car sped forward. A lever hummed as it started downward. The Penguin was activating the weapons systems. Batman grabbed the lever and pushed it back up with all his strength.

"Batman!" The Penguin barked on the monitor. "I know you're not having a swell time, but let me tell you. Taking control of your vehicle, mowing down decent people, and laying the bad vibes squarely on you—makes the hairs in my nose tingle."

Batman was trapped.

The lever that controlled the Batdiscs slammed down again. And this time, no matter how much he tried, Batman couldn't budge it.

Penguin glanced up at his third monitor, the one hooked into cable TV.

"Batman is out of control!" a reporter was shouting. "First he murdered the Ice Princess, and now—"

His reporting was cut mercifully short as one of the Batmobile's Batdiscs thunked him on the side of the head. My, The Penguin thought, he'd always wanted to do something like that. Probably mussed the reporter's hair up no end.

He turned his attention back to the Batmobile.

"Ha!" he said to his camera. "The flimsiest evidence, and all those taterheads turn on you! Hey, just relax, and

I'll take care of the squealing, wretched, pinhead puppets of Gotham.''

He looked out of his driving monitor. Screaming Gothamites were fleeing every which way in front of the marauding Batmobile. But wait! Look at that defenseless grandmother they had left behind. She stared at the onrushing car, frozen with fear. This was the sort of victim The Penguin liked to see.

"Helpless old lady at twelve o'clock!" he announced for Batman's benefit.

The Penguin pressed down on the accelerator.

Something around here still had to control the car, if only so that the vehicle would respond to the remote signals. The Batman just had to think it through, but fast, before The Penguin's command of the Batmobile killed someone.

He pulled open the ceiling panel, revealing a mass of fuses, the real control center of the Batmobile. But which one? He tried to visualize all the charts he'd drawn when he'd helped to design this thing. Third one from the left should do it. Or so he hoped.

Batman reached up and pulled.

The Batmobile squealed to a halt.

The old lady, only a few feet in front of the suddenly still vehicle, ran away at last.

One saved, Batman thought. And one more to go.

CHAPTER
Thirty-Two

The Penguin cackled happily on the monitor. For the merest of instants, Batman thought about disabling the monitor instead.

But that would save his ego, not his life.

"You gotta admit," The Penguin croaked. "I've played this stinking city like a harp from hell!"

Not for long, Batman thought. He drove his fist through the monitor, silencing The Penguin with a shower of sparks. There. Sometimes you just needed to feed your ego.

And maybe there was another way to stop the Batmobile.

He kicked downward with his heel once, twice, three times. There. The floor panel had bent enough for him to pry it up.

He pulled it free, revealing a mass of wires and spinning gears.

He punched down quickly, trusting his glove to protect him from the gears, and popped open the bottom panel so that he could see the spinning ground below. There, mounted to the Batmobile's undercarriage, was some sort of antennae; no doubt the heart of The Penguin's control.

Batman reached down and snapped it in two.

Now it was time to get out of here.

Batman hit the accelerator and shot between two of the police cars and out of Gotham Plaza.

What?

The Penguin couldn't believe it.

"Came this close to a perfect evening!" he cried in anguish. He pounded the controls. "Iced the princess. Blew away Batman. Almost got married. Killed the bitch." He held up two black-gloved fingers. "*This* close!"

But somehow Batman had gotten away. Gotten away! It was enough to sour The Penguin's whole day.

Luckily, he had his other plans to fall back on. The mayor's race, for one. And after that, his masterstroke, so magnificently nasty that he could forget any small failings here.

Not that Gotham City would ever forget. No, he was sure that, once his plans were complete, they'd remember Oswald Cobblepot—forever.

Batman wasn't in the clear yet.

Three police cars had managed to give chase. A couple

of them had cops firing at him. Not that that was a worry. Even a damaged Batmobile was sufficiently bulletproof. But if possible, he needed to shake these cruisers without hurting anybody else.

He rummaged through the exposed wires on the dashboard. That was a second problem; he needed to override whatever damage The Penguin had done to his vehicle, and get the Batmobile's functions operating at a level that would help him with his escape.

He made a sharp right. The cruisers managed to follow. The street narrowed in front of him, into a space so narrow that you could barely call it an alley. Much too narrow for the Batmobile, or the police cruisers. It was time for one of those special Batmobile functions right now.

Batman flipped a switch. Nothing happened. The switch was dead.

But the wires that controlled that switch were still here behind the dashboard. Batman pushed aside the torn instrument panel and quickly pulled the two loose wires out of the mass. He sparked their ends together. Now.

The windshield wipers began to beat back and forth. Not at all what he had wanted.

"That's funny," Batman murmured. How many wires had The Penguin's thugs tampered with? He frowned down at the assembly around. But where could the wires be that he needed?

The alley was coming up fast.

"Now I'm a little worried—" he began. "Oh." There they were.

He connected the right wires this time.

The sides of the Batmobile fell away as the wheels

realigned themselves beneath him, making his vehicle a streamlined bullet of a car, narrow enough to fit through the space immediately ahead—something he called the Batmissile.

They tried to follow, but only succeeded in wedging their vehicle between the walls. From the noise that followed, Batman surmised that the other two cruisers piled into the back of the first.

He was in the clear. He leaned into his turn, and disappeared into darkness.

He just wasn't in the mood.

Max Shreck stood by his side, trying to be cheerful enough for both of them as he guided The Penguin toward the platform where he was scheduled to give his speech.

"—so he survived," Max said dismissively. "Come on, be a mensch. Stand tall—" His voice trailed off as he saw the look The Penguin gave him. Perhaps Max recalled that, the last time Oswald Cobblepot had felt this way, he'd almost bitten off somebody's nose. Of course, since that incident, the lovely Jen seemed to have kept her distance, too. Some women were just too sensitive.

But Penguin couldn't think about women. Now *that* was truly misery! No, all he could think of was Batman—a living, breathing, totally intact Batman.

"He didn't even lose a limb, an eyeball." He sighed at the indignity. "Bladder control!"

Max wouldn't listen. He waved at the cheering crowd in the plaza, and pointed at the latest banner: RECALL THE MAYOR.

Straight and to the point.

"Point is," Max insisted as he waved to the audience, "listen to them. They've lost faith in the old symbols. They're ready to bond with you, the icon of the future." He smiled encouragingly. "If it works, don't fix it—"

Well, yeah, they were yelling for him, weren't they? He could hear a chant rising from the throng. "Os-wald, Os-wald, Os-wald." Yeah. Oswald Cobblepot, hero to the teeming millions of Gotham City. Not the Mayor. Not Batman. Oswald Cobblepot. He stared gloomily at the special deluxe black umbrella he carried for the occasion.

"We'll celebrate tonight," Shreck insisted, "at my annual Max-squerade Ball. Shreck and Cobblepot, the visionary alliance!"

But Penguin's eyes were on the crowd. They were all screaming. They were all screaming for him. More important, a lot of them were women, screaming for him. No, they weren't just women, they were babes; cheap, maybe, tawdry most certainly, but they were *his* babes. Screaming Cobblepot Groupies. It gave him a reason to go on. To think that a poor boy, abandoned by his parents, raised in a rotting exhibit on the edge of the sewers by emperor and king penguins, could get these kind of babes. This was America—truly the land of opportunity!

The Penguin moved to the microphone, and the cheering redoubled. He could feel the adulation of the masses, and it gave him strength. When he spoke, his voice was no longer a simple squawk. Now it was a booming squawk.

"When it came our time to ensure the safety of our city, did the Mayor have a plan?" The Penguin began. "No, he relied on a man. A 'bat' man!"

The crowd screamed their adulation. For The Penguin,

more than just Oswald Cobblepot, abandoned child and sometime crook. No, they screamed for Oswald Cobblepot, supreme ruler of Gotham!

Yes, The Penguin could *really* get into this!

Selina Kyle stood and watched all the hoopla, and all the cheering, for the two men who had tried to kill her.

Max Shreck.

Oswald Cobblepot. A. k. a. The Penguin.

She didn't begrudge them their few, pitiful moments of glory. She wanted them to go as high as this campaign would allow.

The heights, after all, would make their fall so much more satisfying.

Catwoman wasn't playing anymore. It was time for her to sharpen her claws.

CHAPTER
Thirty-Three

Bruce Wayne found himself watching television again, and another of those never-ending media events with The Penguin.

And this time, The Penguin was talking about Batman.

"A ticking time bomb of a costumed freak," the over-blown politician exclaimed to the crowd, "who finally exploded last night, spraying this city with a shrapnel of shame!"

The Penguin was there. The crowd was there. The TV cameras were there. It was time.

Bruce walked over to his aquarium, and reached into the replica of Wayne Manor in the middle of the exotic fish. He fished out a key from an upper bedroom window.

Alfred frowned at the TV. "I'm less worried about this

ghastly, grotesque—more concerned about repairing the Batmobile. It's not as though we can simply bring it to Joe's Body Shop. Is it, sir?''

Bruce glanced up at the butler. Look who was worried about security.

"Hey, who let Vicki Vale into the Batcave?" he asked with a smile and a shake of his head. "I'm sitting there working, I turn around, it's like, 'Oh, hi, Vick. C'mon in.' "

The butler did nothing more than raise an eyebrow. Sometimes, Bruce wondered who exactly was in charge around here.

But there were other, more interesting things to wonder about. "Selina," Bruce mused as he shook the water off his wrist. "More facets than Vicki, huh?" He walked over to an Iron Maiden in another corner of the room. "Funny, but sort of mysterious—"

Alfred nodded curtly. "That's your own affair, sir."

Was it really? Whenever Alfred allowed his employer to have an opinion—rather than curtly commenting upon his mistakes—it meant the butler actually approved of Bruce's latest interest.

And Bruce Wayne always held Alfred's opinions in the highest regard.

"Affair," he murmured. "Yes, maybe—if she—"

He let the rest of the sentence hang as he placed the key in the maiden's lock and turned. It sprang open to reveal its deadly spikes. Bruce stepped inside.

"I believe I'll take the stairs," Alfred commented dryly.

The spikes retreated and the bottom dropped out from under Bruce.

He was on his way to the Batcave.

And The Penguin was on his way to a surprise.

Bruce jumped from the chute that had brought him from the mansion above. He pulled out the recordable CD that he had taken from the Batmobile, and inserted it into his specially modified player.

Alfred came puffing down the stairs behind him. The Penguin was displayed in all his glory on the large monitor that dominated this corner of the cave. He droned on with his never-ending speech.

"You ask, am I up here for personal glory?" The Penguin asked.

That was it, Bruce thought. Keep on talking until I can get the equipment set up properly and Alfred can determine the frequency. He flipped a whole bank of switches.

"Ha!" Cobblepot barked. "I toiled for many years in happy obscurity, beneath your boulevards."

In the meantime, Alfred toiled as well. He sat down at his own console, and punched up the FIND FREQUENCY command. The computers only took a few seconds to respond with FREQUENCY FOUND. They had the signal. Now, all they needed was to make a few minor adjustments, and those modifications Batman had made to the Gotham Plaza public address system should soon become apparent.

"No," The Penguin continued, oblivious to the fun that was to come, "the glory I yearn to recapture is the glory of Gotham!"

Alfred punched in another command, JAM FREQUENCY.

"How can this be accomplished?" The Penguin continued grandly. "I know you're all concerned."

FREQUENCY JAMMED. That's what it said on Alfred's computer.

It was time to play.

The Penguin was on a roll. He had all the birds and babes in Gotham in the palm of his flipper!

"—the glory of Gotham!" he shouted.

Everybody cheered.

"How can this be accomplished?" he called.

"Tell us!" they called back. "We want to know, Oswald!"

"I know you're all concerned," he continued, "and I'll tell you!"

There was no response. His microphone had gone dead.

Certainly, it was only a momentary glitch in the communications system. Max's people would have it fixed in a jiffy. The Penguin decided to repeat the last sentence, just to see if he'd get any results.

"I know—" he began.

His voice boomed back at him: "Hey, just relax and I'll take care of the squealing, wretched, pinhead puppets of Gotham!"

The Penguin stared at the microphone.

"Wait a sec—" he sputtered. "I didn't say that!"

At least, he hadn't said it since last night, when he was talking to Batman.

Last night? Batman?

But nobody could hear his real voice anymore. Instead, his recorded voice boomed on.

"You gotta admit, I've played this stinking city like a harp from hell!"

But those remarks were strictly off the record! Not, of course, that he didn't mean them, but not in front of the babes!

The crowd was booing now, and throwing things! His campaign workers were backing away from him. The Penguin turned and glared at Max. How could he allow something like this to happen?

Perhaps it was time to rethink his campaign.

Bruce Wayne allowed himself a smile.

The crowd was reacting just as he'd hoped they would, angry that The Penguin had deceived them. And The Penguin, not the most stable of individuals, was getting angry right back at them!

What could Bruce do now but raise the stakes?

He punched a series of buttons and placed his palm on the CD, letting the computer single out that special phrase. Here it was.

"This stinking city—" and again, "stinking city—stinking city—stink-stink-stinking city—" Just like a DJ at one of those downtown clubs. Penguin, how do you like that rap?

"—stink-stink—"

Hey, it had a beat. And who said Batman wasn't up-to-date?

The Penguin fell back from the microphone, spinning around, almost losing his balance.

"—stink-stink—stinking city—"

Somebody hit him with a snowball, lettuce, tomatoes.

And the performance went on.

"—stink—stinking—stink—"

It was music to Bruce's ears.

The Penguin had to get out of this place.

He grabbed his umbrella. Now, if he could get the rotor motor working.

But wait! He'd brought the wrong umbrella for escape. Why, after all, would he have to escape from his adoring crowd? The Penguin squawked bitterly. Say something bad about Gotham, belittle the populace a little, and how soon things change!

This black number The Penguin held now had another function entirely.

People threw more things at the stage. And, even worse, some of the missiles were finding The Penguin. Rotten fruit, vegetables, eggs?

"Why is there always someone who brings eggs and tomatoes to a speech?" he cried aloud.

He guessed it was just a part of the American Way. Well, he carried another part of that inalienable dream in his umbrella: the right to bear arms.

He lifted his bumbershoot and sprayed bullets into the crowd.

Turn on me, will you, Gotham City?

Somehow, this just seemed to make the audience more upset. The Penguin decided it was time to head for cooler climes.

He jumped from the stage, heading out of the plaza and toward the park. A number of the good citizens gave chase.

Oh, dear. He didn't want to encourage a mob scene. He

managed to leap a park bench, but the Gothamites were gaining. He turned and gave them another taste of lead.

Still, his machine umbrella didn't have a limitless amount of ammunition. And cops were showing up, returning his fire!

He had to get out of here.

That bridge, ahead, looked awfully familiar. Almost like it was out of a storybook someplace, a quaint stone bridge nestled in the woods above a rushing stream. Except the Penguin thought this particular story was much more personal: He had visions of a baby carriage, and another fall, a long time ago.

The Penguin jumped, losing himself in the icy waters of the river below, and the sewer beyond that he called home.

So much for politics.

Now it was time to get down to his real business.

CHAPTER
Thirty-Four

The Penguin trudged out of the sewer pipe. He was wet, bedraggled, and humiliated, but he was home. He kept his eyes low, partially perhaps from dejection, but also from self-preservation. You never knew quite what the sewers held.

He banged into something. He looked up. It was his rubber-duck boat. Yes, he could use this in his plans, too, those same plans he'd let Max and his own foolishness lead him away from. What did he care about babes? When the time came, The Penguin would take all the babes he wanted, and there would be no one to stop him!

He jumped into the boat and revved it over the sewage lagoon to his arctic island. There, ahead, were the penguins, his penguins, squawking and playing.

The Penguin smiled despite his pain.

"My babies," he murmured. "Did you miss me?"

The penguins seemed to squawk in reply. He drove his duck up to the dock as he saw the first few members of the Red Triangle Circus Gang enter his lair through the main tunnel. He guessed things got a little bit too hot for them, too, after his speech. Or the speech that Batman made for him.

There were debts to be paid, when the time came.

The clown waved and bounded over to The Penguin as he climbed from his craft.

"Great speech, Oswald!" his grease-painted crony said with a laugh. "The way you told those rubes the score!"

Penguin smacked the clown on the head with his umbrella.

"My name's not Oswald," he barked, "it's The Penguin!" Yeah, he thought. That was more like it. "I am not a human being!" he continued. "I'm an animal! Cold blooded! Crank the A.C.!"

He pulled off his tuxedo coat and those damned gloves. Ah, how good it felt for his flippers to be free! It was time to get cold.

"Where's my list?" he demanded. "Bring me the names!"

With that, the Knife Lady entered the lair, carrying a great stack of yellow legal pads with all the information he'd gathered, courtesy of the Hall of Records and the Gotham City phone book.

"It's time!" He chortled with glee, hopping from one foot to the other. For this was the night of Max's party, the social event of the season, and all his victims would be unprotected. Yes, indeed. "Gotham will *never* forget."

He tore off the top page and handed it to the first of his minions, then the second page to another.

"Evan Black," read an acrobat who'd taken a page, "181 Shepard's Lane?"

"Thomas Frankel?" the clown chimed in from the page he now held, "273 Carlton Avenue?"

The Penguin decided he'd better spell it out for all of them.

"These are the firstborn sons of Gotham City!" he cried to the assembled gang. "Like I was! And just like me, a terrible fate waits for them! Tonight, while their parents party, they'll be dreaming away in their safe cribs, their soft beds, and we will snatch them"—he closed his flippers into an approximation of fists—"carry them into the sewer"—he danced merrily over to the water's edge—"and toss them into a deep, dark, watery *grave!*"

Some of the gang members muttered at that. A few even exchanged looks. The acrobat who'd taken the first yellow page looked to his boss.

"Ummm, Penguin?" he said hesitantly. "I mean— kids? Sleeping? Isn't that a little—"

The Penguin lofted his sleek black umbrella and shot the acrobat dead. Not to mention to pieces.

"No," he finished the other's sentence dryly, "it's a *lot.*"

The rest of the Red Triangle Circus Gang managed a

hasty cheer. Good. Showed just what a little well-placed discipline could do.

Not to mention a few well-placed bullets.

There were certain duties a butler never approved of. Still, a duty was a duty, and could not be forgotten until it was fulfilled. So it was that Alfred took the invitation down to the Batcave to remind his employer.

Master Bruce was hard at work on the undercarriage of the Batmobile, which still looked like a total shambles. Alfred would not be surprised if it took weeks to get the vehicle in proper working order.

Alfred cleared his throat. Bruce looked up from his work, and the butler proffered the invitation. He held it as far away from himself as possible. He wished he didn't have to hold it at all.

"Mr. Wayne," Alfred managed. "A reminder. Tonight is that loathsome party, hosted by that failed kingmaker, Max Shreck. May we RSVP in the resounding negative?"

His employer paused for a moment before responding. "I'm tempted, but"—he frowned—"well, it is an occasion for celebration, and—ummmm"—his frown changed to the slightest of smiles—"Selina will probably be there."

Oh, dear. There were certain more important things, then, than snubbing kingmakers.

"Ah," Alfred replied. He regarded his employer for an instant. "Who, may I ask, are you going as?"

But Bruce only smiled enigmatically.

"You'll never guess."

CHAPTER
Thirty-Five

This, at least, would come out right.

These last few days had not been among the best for Max Shreck. First, there was that little altercation with Selina. Unfortunate how Max's temper could sometimes get the better of him. It was very fortunate she survived her tumble from the tower, he supposed, although the fall did seem to have done something to her brain. Perhaps it would be better, after the holiday season was past, to have her removed. Permanently. Except this time Max would have the job done by outside professionals. He was much too big a man to get personally involved in that sort of thing anymore.

And what about The Penguin? Max had thought he had

seen opportunity knocking with the little birdman, but unfortunately, his chosen candidate appeared to have even more screws loose than the average politician. At least now that The Penguin had been disgraced and was the subject of a massive police manhunt, he and his threats were out of Max's life for good.

So now it was time for the big party, time for holiday cheer, time to forget the old and embrace the new. And it was a time for renewal, and a new year to finally get his special power plant under construction.

Yes, there had been some pitfalls along the way, but Max had successfully avoided them all. And he wanted to show he was still here, and still kicking. What better way to do that than hold his annual Max-squerade in the recently bombed department store, patched up and lit like a night-club for this occasion?

Sometimes, Max was so clever he surprised even himself.

He had dressed himself in a special turban headdress for tonight's party. Just like a swami who knows all. And the guests started to arrive in droves. He saw someone dressed as the leaning tower of Pisa, another dressed as the sinking of the Titanic.

But, with all the varied costumes, it was telling that there wasn't a single penguin. How fickle the public was in Gotham City!

Max climbed up on the platform. It was time for the party to begin.

"Attention, shoppers!" he called into the microphone.

A number of the guests laughed appreciatively. They'd better, with what this was costing Max. But, hey, the goodwill this generated, especially among certain Gotham City departments and commissions! A party was always worthwhile when it got officials to look the other way.

"Like this splendid department store," Max continued, "Gotham can quickly bounce back from the tumult, the sturm and drang of the past days." He lifted both his hands above his head and waved to the crowd. "So deck the halls and shake your booties!"

The band behind him launched into a tune with a heavy beat, and a number of the guests obligingly crowded the makeshift dance floor.

Max spotted the mayor, wearing a Julius Caesar toga, complete with rubber knife handles and a lot of fake blood. Max lifted his drink in a toast to the mayor with his best "forgive me" smile. The Mayor nodded noncommittally. Still, the very fact that His Honor had attended meant he realized how much he needed Max Shreck's money, power, and influence.

Max turned to stare at the another newcomer who stood out in the crowd.

It was Bruce Wayne. Obviously. Because Bruce Wayne had come dressed as himself.

Well, no matter what Wayne decided to do, Max decided he should be the gracious host. Especially considering Wayne's money, power, and influence.

"Ingenious costume," Max remarked as he shook Wayne's hand. "Let me guess—trust fund goody-goody?"

But Wayne wasn't in the mood for banter. "Of course you're feeling fine," he replied with a frown. "You almost made a monster the mayor of Gotham City."

What was this Bruce Wayne talking about? Didn't he realize all that Penguin business was part of the past?

Max took a deep breath. "I am the light of this city. And I am its mean, twisted soul. Does it really matter who's the mayor?"

Wayne regarded him coolly. "You know what? It does to me."

"Yawn," Max replied. It was time to find more interesting conversation.

There was something about Max Shreck's money-can-fix-anything attitude that brought out Bruce's most self-righteous instincts. He found the man extremely unpleasant. For a moment Bruce Wayne thought it was a mistake to come here.

Then he saw Selina.

She wasn't dressed in costume either, unless her costume was Selina Kyle. Heck, with a face and figure like that, why should she want to hide it?

Bruce quickly crossed the dance floor in her direction. She was talking to Chip Shreck, who was dressed like some soldier from ancient Rome. Or, rather, Chip was talking to her.

"Selina," Chip said in what almost sounded like awe. "Ms. Kyle. May I have this—"

Bruce stepped in, and Selina looked at him as if Chip Shreck didn't even exist.

He smiled at her. She smiled back. The band started to play something slow. Somehow, they were in each other's arms and dancing.

"Sorry about yesterday," he said quickly. "Some big

deal came together—'' No, that wasn't what he'd told Alfred to say. ''—uh, no, fell through, and—'' Or was that what he told the butler to say? Bruce couldn't remember.

Selina replied before he could get into further trouble. ''It's okay.'' She shrugged. ''I had to go home. Feed my cat.''

Bruce couldn't believe it. He looked into her eyes. ''No hard feelings?''

She pressed close to him. She looked up and smiled.

''Actually—semihard, I'd say.''

Oh. Bruce took a step away, suddenly embarrassed. If only he didn't find Selina Kyle so attractive.

But he did.

Selina did an amazingly slow pirouette before him, graceful and sexy at the same time.

''There's a big, comfy, California king over in Bedding,'' she suggested. ''What say we—''

''You mean,'' Bruce asked with a certain irony, ''take off our costumes?''

Selina's answering laugh sounded more sad than happy. ''I guess I'm sick of wearing masks.''

''Same here,'' he agreed. ''So why did you come tonight?''

She shook her head. ''You first.''

He drew her close again. ''To see you.''

She didn't reply for a long moment. When she did, he heard that same sadness in her voice.

''That's lovely, and I really wish I could say the same, but—I came for Max.''

Bruce almost stopped dancing. Max Shreck? Was there

something going on in front of him that he hadn't even seen? An office flirtation, or maybe even romance?

"You don't mean—you and Max?" he asked tentatively.

This time Selina's laugh let him know he couldn't be further from the truth. She shook her head.

"*This* and Max," she explained.

She reached into her purse and pulled out a derringer.

CHAPTER
Thirty-Six

Bruce pushed the derringer back in her bag and continued to dance. Selina was surprised she had even shown it to him. She had meant to keep her gun a secret from everyone. But then she had told him about it, straight out. There was something about Mr. Bruce Wayne, something mysterious, but something that made her want to trust him at the same time.

She looked at the surprise on his face, and decided to talk before he did.

"Now," she began, "don't give me a killing-Max-won't-solve-anything speech, because it will. Aren't you tired of this sanctimonious robber baron always coming out on top? When he should be six feet under?"

Bruce shook his head ruefully. "Hey, look, I'm sure

you have plenty of reasons to hate your boss, but—'' He threw his hands in the air, as if he didn't know the answer either. "Jesus, Selina, you're not the judge or the jury. I mean, just who do you think you are?"

She looked back at him thoughtfully, and a little sadly. Before the Ice Princess had died, she could have told him. She had so much anger against so many things; and that anger had come out as Catwoman. But now?

"I don't know anymore, Bruce," she said, and she could hear her own despair.

Still they danced, swirling around the floor to that slow, sad song. She looked overhead and saw mistletoe. She leaned forward and gave Bruce a gentle kiss that somehow felt sad as well.

"A kiss under the mistletoe," she said, repeating another's words. "Mistletoe can be deadly, if you eat it—"

Bruce looked at her, and told her other words she knew.

"But a kiss can be even deadlier, if you mean—it."

He stumbled over the last word, as if he had guessed the same thing she had.

They both spoke at once.

"You're her?" he said at the same time as she asked "You're him?"

They were. They both knew it in the instant they spoke.

He was Batman?

And she was Catwoman. But who would believe it?

Besides the two of them.

Bruce very gently undid the cuff of her blouse, and pulled back her sleeve. His hand on her skin was almost a caress as he felt her upper arm.

"The burn I gave you," he said. She could hear regret in his voice.

But she needed proof as well, she realized, as she undid the bottom button of his shirt and felt along his stomach muscles. There was the row of scabs.

"The puncture wounds I gave you," she replied. She sighed. This was all too much for her. "Oh, God," she whispered, afraid to say what came next. "Does this mean we have to start fighting now?"

Bruce's only answer was to pull her closer. She hugged him tight. She was scared. She imagined they both were.

"What do we do?" she asked after a moment.

"I don't know," Bruce replied. "Until we figure it out, let's—let's keep dancing."

For the moment, Selina realized, that was fine with her.

Now this was really more like it!

The Penguin cackled as the dust and dancers settled around them. Nothing like a nice little explosion to shake them up. Well, tonight, The Penguin would make them pay!

Bits of the floor sailed back to earth.

People screamed.

Pieces of ceiling rained down around them.

People fainted.

Parts of other things fell down, too. Some of these had once been costumes; or what had been inside the costumes.

People ran.

The Penguin made a small bow from within his duck-mobile. "You didn't invite me, so I crashed."

The four penguins he'd brought along squawked approval.

His Honor the Mayor stepped forward. The Penguin had to admit, he was a snappy dresser. Of course, The Penguin always was a sucker for a toga.

"What do you want, Penguin?" His Honor demanded.

The Penguin pushed him out of the way. He had no more time for mayors. He had much more important things to announce. He looked out at the assembled party-goers to make certain he had their total attention.

"Right now, my troops are fanning out across town, for your children!" He paused to allow the audience to gasp. "Yes, for your firstborn sons. The ones you left defenseless, at home, so you could dress up like jerks, get juiced, and dance, badly!"

He turned to a certain older firstborn kid.

"I've personally come for Gotham's favorite son—Mr. Chip Shreck!"

Even more people gasped. A couple even screamed.

Ah, violence, threats, murder. Why did The Penguin ever leave those things he was so good at?

Well, all that was sewage under the bridge. Because with dear Chip, and hundreds of other Chips from all over town, The Penguin was getting back into murder in a big way.

Hey, this was even *better* than being mayor!

This was terrible!

The two of them had gone down together when the floor exploded. Bruce had been underneath, to cushion the worst of her fall. By the time they had both regained their feet, The Penguin had managed to take Chip Shreck captive.

Selina turned away from The Penguin and his goon.

"Bruce," she said. "We have to do something!"

But Bruce was gone.

CHAPTER
Thirty-Seven

M ax stared in horror as his son was taken hostage.
"You're coming with me, you Great White
Dope," The Penguin declared with perverse glee. "To
die, way down in the sewer."

Max almost stopped breathing. For the first time that he
could remember, he was truly frightened.

"Not Chip!" he called out, surprised how strong his
voice still sounded. "Please! Penguin—if you have one
iota of human feeling, you'll take me instead."

The Penguin turned to Max and sneered.

"I don't," he barked. "So, no."

But Max knew he had to save his son. He threw himself
toward The Penguin's huge duck.

"I'm the one you want!" he insisted. "Penguin, please! Ask yourself!" He pointed to himself. "Isn't it Max Shreck who manipulated and betrayed you? Isn't it Max, not Chip, whom you want to see immersed to his eyeballs in raw sewage?"

The Penguin paused to consider Max's plea.

"Okay, you have a point. Plus the hysterics are getting on my nerves."

"Let Knute Rockne live for now." The thug removed his gun from Chip's face. Cautiously, the younger Shreck backed away. He looked to his father, as if he was sure that Max had a plan.

Max's relief at seeing Chip freed was soon replaced by dismay at having the gun put to his own head.

Max looked at the birds around him. The penguins were not only wearing funny-looking helmets, they were armed! And the way they were pointing those guns, they looked ready to shoot into the crowd.

The whole world went gray as four smoke bombs went off simultaneously.

What was he doing? He wasn't the self-sacrificing sort. Well, he had sacrificed himself for his son. It was a shock, but Max realized he did have a shred of human decency.

And that decency would be the death of him.

"Dad!" he heard Chip call from somewhere in the crowd. But he had no reply as the smoke closed over him.

All Max could do was cough.

And now the wonderful Penguin's plan took shape. He could see it now, all the talented members of the Red

Triangle Circus Gang tumbling their ways into the homes of Gotham's firstborn sons.

Here's one pretty scene, in a precious bathroom, the child's own. The walls are covered with sheep, daisies, and the letters of the Alphabet; so cute it could make you sick. A toddler, a firstborn toddler, stands there, making faces at himself in a mirror. He's giggling. It's the funniest thing that he's ever seen.

But uh-oh. What's this but his nannie's voice, coming sternly through the bathroom door.

"Billy," she says. "If you're not brushing, I'll tell your mama!"

He's in trouble now.

The toddler looks back in the mirror, and sees that he's not alone.

His visitor, the Knife Lady, grabs him before he can scream, her hand clamped firmly over his mouth. And away they go.

Soon, this toddler will never get into trouble again.

Too traumatic for you? All right, let's postulate another small drama. A darling little boy sits at the windowsill, staring out with wonder at the night sky. But who should appear at his window but a happy clown?

The boy claps his hands in delight. "Finally, the tooth fairy!" And, now that that's all established, he gets down to business. "What do I get?"

The clown, who can see that the darling boy has indeed lost one of his upper front teeth, smiles even more broadly than before.

"Why, the ride of your life," he says. "Hey, c'mon, little guy—"

The clown reaches out a hand and the little boy takes it, ecstatic that he is going on an adventure. No need to tell him that it will be his last.

And look over there, in that plush nursery. The infant boy sleeps soundly in his expensive crib, custom-built, no doubt, with the lumber from some endangered tree. But one of our acrobats vaults through the window, then scoops up the child in one fluid motion. The child sleeps on as the acrobat vaults back out. An alarm wails, did you say? Perhaps so, but it is too late, far too late for all of Gotham City.

And so it goes. House after house after house. Firstborn son after firstborn son.

And soon, the big kaboom! All of Gotham's firstborn brats, sunken and strangled.

It was enough to make The Penguin breathless.

CHAPTER
Thirty-Eight

M ax had never known this kind of misery before.
The Penguin had put him in a cage, but that wasn't bad enough. The cage was hung immediately above a pond full of brown and acrid goo. Max half expected to choke to death on the fumes! And it was cold down here, too! That huge air conditioner was turned so high that there was ice everywhere; and somehow the sparks from the generator next to it did nothing to warm the place back up. Max didn't want to know what was in this goo to keep it from freezing, but he had the feeling that the liquid could ruin his pants, perhaps even eat them away.

The Penguin's men had given him a ratty blanket to

throw over his shoulders, but all it did was keep his shivers to a minimum. He'd die of exposure if The Penguin didn't kill him first.

But, then, he was quite sure The Penguin was going to kill him.

The Penguin pranced about before him, a long black umbrella in either hand.

"Ooh," the bird man almost sang, "this is gonna be good!"

He turned to Max. "To cut down a whole crop of Gotham's most promising, before their prime—" He pointed his umbrella toward a spot past Max, and a whole lake full of some liquid even more vile than that surrounding the businessman.

"How do I lure them in, you ask?" The Penguin continued rhetorically. He popped open a red and white umbrella. Max flinched backwards. But instead of bullets or knives, this bumbershoot transformed itself into a charming miniature merry-go-round. The music was hauntingly familiar. Maybe it was a lullabye.

The Penguin held the charming miniature above him, and waved for a pack of imaginary kids to follow. "A little Pied Penguin action," he explained. "And you get to watch them all sink in a deep puddle of your industrial by-products." He turned back to Max. "Then you join them. Tragic irony or poetic justice? You tell me."

But Max was too cold to care.

It was a circus train from hell.

The odd collection of circus wagons wound its way through the early morning streets of Gotham City. They were bright wagons, painted blue and red and yellow, cheerful circus colors.

But each of these old and cheerful wagons was a cage, its sides filled with iron bars. And behind these bars were children; four or five to a wagon. All boys, all the firstborn sons of Gotham, destined to be The Penguin's victims. Or so he planned.

Occasionally, a baby's cry would break through the near silence. Most of the boys seemed too terrified to speak. Somebody called weakly for help. An acrobat leaned down and told him, "Shut up and enjoy the choo-choo ride. Or you'll be sorry."

The locomotive stopped, waiting for the next delivery. At the wheel, the Organ Grinder impatiently plucked his monkey from his shoulder. He looked back at the collection of acrobats, jugglers, and clowns aiding him in his work.

"Would you hurry up loading those kids already?" he yelled. It looked like he was getting tired of this whole trip.

A shadow fell across his face, startling the driver out of his boredom. His monkey screamed. He looked up as Batman yanked the Organ Grinder from his seat.

He'd make sure the thug got a little action. And after he was done here, he had a short appointment with some acrobats, jugglers, and clowns.

The Penguin had to get this just right. No use frightening the little darlings before they all drowned horribly in the toxic ooze. He pirouetted with his colorful umbrella, ready to lead his firstborn victims in a merry dance.

"This way, kiddies," he said in his most inviting tones. "Jump right in!"

Of course, if the kids disagreed, he'd just machine-gun a few of them to get them started.

He paused as he heard a shriek from the entryway to his lair. He stopped the music as he saw the Organ Grinder's monkey scamper down the stairs toward him. A smelly, noisy creature, the monkey, not at all as regal as an emperor penguin; but why was the monkey here without the Organ Grinder?

"So, where are the kids?" he demanded of the beast. "Don't tell me they stopped at McDonald's?"

"Boss!" The clown pointed. "He's got a note!"

Indeed, the filthy little creature did clutch a piece of paper in its fingers. The Penguin snatched it away and uncrumpled the page.

" 'Dear Penguin,' " he read. " 'The children regret they are unable to attend. Have a disappointing day. Batman.' "

What?

No children? It took The Penguin a moment to come to grips with this. And it would take him more than a minute to control his anger. If he could just get that Bat in the sights of his umbrella. But no, where was a hero when you wanted to kill him? Nowhere to be found!

Well, The Penguin would just have to kill something else. He glared down at the monkey. The beast looked up at him, hopping and dancing across the icy floor.

"You're the messenger," he reminded himself. "It doesn't make sense to shoot the messenger."

He grabbed his second umbrella, the one loaded with

bullets, and turned to pump twenty rounds into the Fat Clown.

There. That felt much better.

And The Penguin wasn't finished yet. He had more plans. Bigger plans. Deadlier plans.

But, this time, he'd use somebody he could trust.

CHAPTER
Thirty-Nine

Why hadn't he just done this in the first place? After all, he'd been planning this campaign for years, designing the special headgear, fitting the guns and heavy weaponry so that they could be operated by birds. But he'd gotten sidetracked by dreams of personal glory, or personalized revenge. But these dreams had depended on outside factors; people and events that The Penguin could not control.

He looked out at his troops, over a hundred strong. It had taken The Penguin and the remaining members of the Red Triangle Circus Gang close to a whole day to outfit them all, but it had been worth it, for they'd finished their work just before Christmas Eve.

And what next? The Penguin had thought about this speech long and hard, for it would lead to his greatest moment!

"My penguins," he began solemnly. "We stand at a great threshold. It's okay to be scared. Many of you won't be coming back."

He had to stop and wipe away a tear. Yes, this was his day of glory, or, as he liked to think of it, Operation Penguin Storm. It was inevitable, he guessed, that it would come to this, especially after his years of grueling study led him to discover the exact pitch and frequency that would cause penguins to follow his every command. That was one advantage to spending years in the sewers—it gave you plenty of time for research. Sure, his troops would be little more than zombies to The Penguin's radio signals, but his cause was just. Not to mention incredibly bloody.

But The Penguin had to complete his stirring address. "Thanks to Batman," he continued, "the time has come to punish all God's chillun—first, second, third and fourth-born!" He laughed grandly. "Why be biased? Male and female, hell—the sexes are equal with their erogenous zones blown sky high!"

He looked over to the control center. There was the Poodle Lady, at the controls, beneath the banks of monitors scavenged from both the old Arctic World pavilions and numerous diverse sources, relaying those fine video signals, from cameras liberated from some of the finer automatic tellers and convenience stores in all of Gotham. And those monitors showed every corner of the sleeping city.

But if the city was sleeping now, soon it would be dead.

"Forward, march!" The Penguin declared. "The liberation of Gotham has begun!"

The whole penguin army swiveled in unison as the Poodle Lady twisted the appropriate knob at the controls. She flipped a switch, and the penguins started to march in step toward the large sewer pipe, and the city beyond.

Penguin had to wipe away another tear.

"The Grinch just *stole* Christmas," he announced to those few, pitiful humans who remained. "I'm gonna kill it, barbecue it, chop it up, and chew its bones!"

Yes, The Penguin thought, smacking his lips.

Pure chewing satisfaction.

The Batmobile might be down, but there was more than one way to patrol Gotham City. Especially when your prey was a creature like The Penguin.

Batman drove the Batskiboat down Gotham River and into the main conduit of the sewers. This would be the first real test of his new vehicle, a sleek, compact black craft designed along the same lines as the Batmobile, a combination of speedboat and jet-ski.

The sewers were dark and vast, and changes over the years had made it virtually impossible to map them from city records. The Penguin might have been able to hide down here for years. But now Batman knew where to look.

Alfred had picked up a signal, similar to the one The Penguin had used on the Batmobile. It seemed that the birdman was again trying his tricks with remote control. But Batman would turn those tricks around, and The Penguin's final fate would be anything but remote.

Batman looked down at a small screen before him. The glowing dot was getting closer. He picked up the phone that connected him with the Batcave.

"I'm homing in on the signal's origin," he announced.

"Ready when you are," Alfred replied. The butler was once again in charge of the computers.

The glowing dot reached the center of the screen and began to flash with twice the intensity. The Penguin's control center was just ahead.

"Got the coordinates," Batman added. "They're—"

He turned his boat around a corner in the sewer pipe. There, in the glow of his headlight, were half a dozen penguins.

Penguins? As Batman scanned the group, he noticed that all the birds were strangely outfitted as well, all wearing odd helmets and carrying what looked like miniature bazookas.

This was what The Penguin controlled. The birds raised their weapons at the approaching boat. It was time for some evasive action.

He gunned the jet motor as he turned the boat to follow the curve of the sewer pipe. The boat rocketed forward, rising from the water and climbing the curve until Batman hung upside down for an instant from the top of the pipe.

The penguins' missiles exploded harmlessly below.

Batman continued his circumnavigation of the sewer pipe, bringing the craft back into the water on the far side of his adversaries. In an instant, the penguins were out of firing range; in another instant, they were out of sight.

"As I was saying—" Batman continued.

He quickly gave the butler the proper coordinates, along with a few final instructions.

Now they could put The Penguin away for good.

All my children, The Penguin thought, marching bravely down the streets of Gotham City, about to blow the city to holy hell. They'd teach the sanctimonious citizens a thing or two—or at least those who were left alive.

He stared up at the monitors, and saw all but one of his units already in place. The last group had delayed by some small disturbance in the sewer tunnels, but even they were climbing from their designated manhole to take up their position outside Gotham Plaza.

The Poodle Lady looked up at the big clock. Everything was right on schedule!

"Ten," the Poodle Lady began her countdown, "nine—"

Penguin could barely contain his enthusiasm. "The Christmas Eve of Destruction!" he chortled. This would let Gotham know how he really felt about the holidays!

"Eight," his assistant continued. "Seven."

The Penguin couldn't help it! He felt like singing!

"Silent night, violent night," he began.

"All is shrill," the Poodle Lady chimed in, "all is blight!"

The Penguins were in position. Larry instructed them to angle their bazookas for maximum destruction of the stores and the last-minute shoppers.

This time, The Penguin was going to give Gotham the biggest Christmas light of all!

CHAPTER
Forty

Alfred sat at the console, ready for his employer's instructions.

"Twenty-eight degrees west," Batman repeated, double-checking the coordinates. "Shall we?"

Alfred typed the appropriate command into the console before him.

FREQUENCY JAMMED, the monitor replied.

The Penguin couldn't take his eyes off the video screens. This was the kind of program that really sucked you in. One final command, and Gotham City would become Götterdämmerung!

"Ah, Gotham," he mused gleefully. "You wouldn't put me on a pedestal, so I'm laying you on a slab!"

The Poodle Lady coughed. She threw a switch, then a second and a third. She seemed to be having a little trouble.

"Well, um, funny thing" she remarked in a very tentative tone, "your penguins—they're not responding to your launch command. In fact"—she flinched before she continued—"they're kind of turned around now—like someone jammed our signal—"

The Penguin stared at her. Jammed? "But who could have—" He paused as he thought of the obvious answer. "No, don't say it."

The Poodle Lady nodded rapidly, her eyes on The Penguin's deadly umbrella.

"My lips are sealed," she agreed.

Wait a moment. That momentary distraction, down in the sewers. Could it be? The Penguin moved forward to the consoles, punching buttons. Not in that pipe, no.

There!

He punched another quick succession of controls, and every screen in front of him showed it. Some kind of boat!

"I'm starting," The Penguin remarked very softly, "just starting, to lose my temper, now."

He grabbed a fresh umbrella and ran for the Duck vehicle.

Max couldn't believe it.

He had spent hours down here, maybe even days, hanging in the cage, dozing from time to time with his arms around the bars. He had thought it was hopeless, only a matter of time before he was killed along with any number of others.

But instead, he had seen not one but two of The Penguin's master plans brilliantly foiled. And The Penguin, so sure of himself before, seemed to have forgotten everything, except revenge. And that everything included Max.

Max had to rouse himself from his stupor. Maybe, with The Penguin gone, there was some way Max could get out of here as well.

The Penguin jumped into his strange Duck vehicle, only a few feet away from Max's cage.

The Penguin steered his contraption out of the sewer and up the stairs!

But Max didn't have any time to worry about what made that duck move. The Penguin was gone, and the key—and freedom—were within easy reach.

Max bent down and grabbed the key from the Organ Grinder's monkey and quickly unlocked himself.

He had to get out of here, back to the surface, before The Penguin had any thoughts about returning. He took a step toward the stairs, and felt something wrap around his other leg.

He looked down.

It was a very fancy whip—a cat-o'-nine-tails.

He grabbed the fallen Fat Clown's gun as he fell into the water.

Batman had almost reached The Penguin's lair.

But something was moving up ahead. He could see a new blip on his screen, a thermal image of what lay ahead. It wasn't a boat exactly. The vehicle ahead appeared to be shaped like a large rubber duck, and it was headed for the surface.

His boat reached a fork in the pipes. Batman turned

sharply, entering the sewer main that angled up toward the surface.

Where Penguins go, Bats can follow.

He had reached the top of Arctic World, the grand and glorious exhibition site of yesteryear, which, more important to The Penguin, held a door that led outside, beyond the sewers, where he might get lost in the great mass of Gotham City. The Penguin laughed as he steered the Duck into the lake beyond the exhibit. He'd steal away to plan another day—

He stopped laughing at the sound of breaking glass. Something was plowing through the top of the old Arctic World.

Something like that damned Batskiboat!

It flew through the air, straight for him. It was going to land on top of him.

The Penguin had to get out of here.

If there was any time.

His craft had stopped. His aim had been perfect, crashing into The Penguin's escape vehicle. But what had happened to The Penguin?

Batman popped open the cockpit and climbed out. He looked beneath his craft for some sign of the bird-man, a bit of soiled coat, perhaps, or a piece of an umbrella.

He saw movement from the corner of his eye.

The Penguin was on top of him!

The bird-man wrapped his legs around Batman's neck, pecking at his cowl, stabbing with the tip of his umbrella. Batman staggered under the weight.

"I think you're jealous—" Penguin declared between pecks, "that I'm a genuine freak—and you have to wear a mask!"

Batman shifted his weight, trying to throw off his assailant. "Maybe you're right," he replied.

The Penguin obligingly jumped away.

"But in the end," the bird-man remarked as he lifted his sleek, black weapon, "all that counts is, 'Who's holding the umbrella?' "

The Penguin pressed the umbrella handle, and a long blade sprang out from the other end, transforming it into a sword.

It was time for Batman to pull out his own weapon. A small, black, palm-sized electronic device featuring a button.

The Penguin's already small eyes narrowed. What was Batman up to? The bird-man circled the Batman warily, keeping his distance.

The Penguin paused abruptly, looking beyond his foe.

"My babies—" he whispered.

Batman risked a look, and saw a whole army of penguins waddling toward the Arctic World. Out of The Penguin's control, they had returned to the place they knew.

The Penguin yelled and lunged forward with his sword. Batman easily avoided the stab, but in his surprise let go of his own weapon.

The Penguin cackled, snatching the weapon from the ground. He grinned at Batman as he held the button out in his foe's direction, and pressed down hard.

Two panels in the Batman's boat fell away, releasing a crowd of bats. Confused bats, agitated bats, locked in an enclosed space for far too long. They flew right for The Penguin and the high-pitched signal button he still held in his hand.

"Ah, you brought your in-laws!" The Penguin remarked as he swatted at them with his umbrella. "I'm sure, once you get to know them—"

But the bats were clustering around him now and the signal that called to them. There were too many of them. He staggered backward, onto the pathway that led to the Arctic World exhibit, running now, trying to escape the circling mammals.

He screamed as he crashed through the glass and fell, back into his lair.

CHAPTER
Forty-One

The bats wouldn't leave him alone!

He had smashed through the old observation window. The glass had cut him in a dozen places, adding to his exhaustion. And the bats were everywhere, swooping, chattering. They were even worse than monkeys!

He looked below, and saw the moat around the old Penguin island coming up fast. He was going to hit hard. Well, the bats couldn't follow him there!

He splashed into the moat, letting himself sink all the way to the bottom.

Batman looked down at the Arctic World exhibit below. The Penguin was nowhere to be seen. But there were two others down there, struggling; Max Shreck and—Catwoman. He'd have to take care of that in a moment. But first, he had to deal with an army of heavily armed penguins.

He moved quickly back to his boat, and used his phone to tell Alfred to stop jamming the signals.

Alfred complied.

The penguins' helmets clicked and hummed. They turned, lifting their bazookas aloft, aimed now for the rotting remains of the rest of the old exhibition—crumbling cages from an old zoo, weathered concession stands with a bit of bright paint remaining here and there, benches and fences that had collapsed long ago.

Another command came through, and the penguins fired together, a grand trajectory of missiles arcing high overhead to fall into the exhibits beyond.

The exposition exploded, full of sound and light for one final time.

She finally had Max Shreck where she wanted him. Alone, in this crumbling exhibit. The world was exploding outside, and the heat seemed to be melting the ice around them. The water level was rising, making the island that she and Max shared smaller by the minute. There was no way for him to escape.

"I don't know what you want," he pleaded, doing his best to smile, "but I know I can get it for you with a minimum of fuss."

He waited for her to suggest something. She didn't.

"Money?" he suggested for her. She didn't react.

"Jewels?" was his next suggestion. But she didn't want that either.

"A very big ball of string?" he asked in desperation.

Well, she supposed she might as well tell him.

"Your blood, Max."

He grew even paler than he had been before.

"M-my blood?" he sputtered. "I—I gave at the office."

"A half pint," Catwoman purred. "I want gallons." She curled her whip around his neck with a flick of her wrist. It was time for Max Shreck to have a little date with that big humming generator.

But Max didn't want to go. "Let's make a deal," he continued feverishly as she literally dragged him along. "*Other* than my blood, what can I offer—"

"Sorry, Max." She thought of that trip out the window during the snowstorm. She certainly hoped he pictured it as well.

"A die for a die," she added, dragging him so that he might have reached out and touched the wheezing generator. The melting ice seemed to have affected it as well. It was definitely laboring now, shooting out a whole, steady stream of sparks.

"Either you've caught a cold," Max replied, "or you're planning to kill me."

Smart boy. All she needed to do was ground dear Max properly, and he should go up in sparks as well.

A rope appeared nearby, dropping down from the dome above. A moment later Batman dropped in as well.

Max whimpered and crawled toward him.

"You're not saving one life," Max called out, "you're saving a city and its way of life!"

Batman drop-kicked him into the generator.

Max yelped as he bounced off. Just a small shock this time. A taste, Catwoman hoped, of things to come.

Batman turned to Max. Sometimes, she had to admit, she liked his style.

"First," he said to the businessman, "you're going to shut up. Then you're going to turn yourself in."

What? This was what she got for getting involved with this sort of goody-goody!

"Don't be naive!" she demanded. "The law doesn't apply to people like him." She paused and looked Batman in the eyes. "Or us."

But Batman shook his head. "Wrong on both counts."

He reached out to take Max.

No. Catwoman wouldn't let that creep get away. She cartwheeled straight at Batman, delivering a swift kick to his abdomen. He flew backwards, falling.

"Why are you doing this?" he asked as he picked himself up. "We could drop him off at the city jail, then go home together—"

As if it could be as simple as that! Couldn't he understand?

"I'm not a house cat," she began pleadingly.

Batman started to smile. She couldn't stand that.

She lashed out with her claws, scratching Batman's face. He pivoted away from her talons, punching out with his fist to push her beyond arm's reach.

"I won't declaw you," Batman explained. "Just watch where you sharpen those things."

Catwoman stared at him. If only she didn't have to deal with Max. But she did, and Batman stood in the way.

"Don't you see," Batman pleaded. "We're the same. Split down the middle." He reached out a gloved hand toward her.

"Just like in a fairy tale," she agreed. "I could live with you in your castle forever after."

If only, she thought, there wasn't this other thing I have to do first.

She leaned forward. She longed for the sweetness of his kiss.

She gave him a head-butt instead.

He reeled backward.

"I just couldn't live with myself," she admitted.

"Selina?" Max remarked as the light suddenly dawned upon him. "Selina Kyle? You're fired!" He looked over at the recovering Batman. "And Bruce—Bruce Wayne? Why are you dressed up as Batman?"

Catwoman replied. "He *is* Batman, you moron."

But Max had a gun in his hand.

"Was," he corrected.

He shot at the rising Batman, catching him in the side of the neck. Batman fell to his knees as Max turned the gun on Catwoman.

Where did he get the gun? She should have been watching Max, not arguing with Bruce. Corn dog—

She stopped herself. That was Selina Kyle's thinking. That was her past. For better or worse, Catwoman would have to face the gun.

She sauntered toward him.

"You killed me," she said demurely, "Batman killed

me, The Penguin killed me. Three lives down. Got enough bullets to finish me off?''

"One way to find out," Max replied. He squeezed the trigger.

One bullet hit her arm. Another ripped into her thigh. She kept on walking. She pulled off her hood.

"Four, five," she remarked. "Still alive."

She was bleeding, but she couldn't feel it.

She pulled out her stun gun. She was going to finish this if it was the last thing she would ever do.

Selina had been shot. Twice.

Batman pulled off his own mask, trying to stanch the blood on his wounded neck. He told himself it wasn't much more than a flesh wound. No matter how bad it was, he had to stop Max before he killed Selina.

He tried to get to his feet, but he was too dizzy.

"Selina—" he managed, "please stop."

Max fired again, hitting her other leg. She kept on coming. He shot one more time, blowing away the barrel of her weapon. Sparks flew from what remained in her hand.

She kept on walking, a little shakier now.

"Six, seven," she managed, "all good girls go to—"

Max aimed at her chest and pulled the trigger. No more bullets.

"Hmm," Selina remarked casually, "two lives left. Think I'll save one for next Christmas. Meantime, how about a kiss, Santy Claus?"

The once-powerful Max Shreck was actively whimpering by now. He stepped back, knocking against the generator.

Selina placed the stun gun in her mouth like some electronic pacifier, then grabbed Max, hugging him close.

"What are you—" Max screamed.

She leaned her head forward as if to kiss him as she drove her talons into the generator's open fuse box. Both their bodies jumped as the electricity arced through them.

Bruce managed to stand as the two others were lost beneath a shower of sparks.

Commissioner Gordon looked out over Gotham Plaza. It was a happy scene for Christmas Eve, as all the stolen children were matched up with their anxious parents, with the help of the police and some mayoral aides. And, of course, the services of Batman.

It had been a strange night. Only a few minutes before, reports had come through about groups of penguins wandering around sporting strange helmets and carrying weapons. But the patrol cars hadn't been able to find a thing. Probably somebody's idea of a joke. It was amazing what Christmas brought out in some people.

The lights dimmed all around them. Were they going to have a blackout? For some reason, the Batsignal blinked to life in the sky for an instant, then was gone.

The lights came back, and this time, the Christmas tree lights came on as well. Parents and children cheered.

Gordon frowned. They had almost lost power in all of Gotham City.

Could Max Shreck have been right about his crazy power plant scheme?

Gordon would be glad when this Christmas Eve was over.

* * *

Bruce heard a high scream of joy come from beneath the sparks. The cry sounded like a cat.

He stumbled forward. He saw a body on the floor.

"Se-li-na Kyle," he called. There was no answer.

He moved forward, through the rising mist that formed when the sparks hit the surrounding mist. There was only one body here, and that belonged to Max Shreck. He was quite dead.

He took a step away. The generator had stopped. Somehow, the lights were still working, but the air-conditioning was gone. It was getting hotter in here by the minute.

He turned as he heard a voice behind him.

"Gotta crank the A.C. Stuffy in here."

It was The Penguin, risen from the sewers.

CHAPTER
Forty-Two

The Penguin looked terrible.

His soiled clothing was soaked and torn, his face and hands bleeding. He supported himself by using two umbrellas as crutches. He seemed to be sweating, too, as he struggled over to the air conditioner, not even aware that someone else was present.

The generator explosion had ignited some of the upper parts of the display. Fiery rubble fell from above. The Penguin dodged the flaming debris as he tossed away one umbrella to free a flipper. He fiddled with the dials on a singed air conditioner. It didn't respond; it was as dead as the generator.

He turned and saw Batman.

"Without the mask," he croaked, "you're drop-dead

handsome." He grunted as he raised his umbrella. "So drop dead."

He pressed the handle. The top of the umbrella transformed itself into a whirling merry-go-round.

"Shit," The Penguin muttered. "Picked the cute one. Heat's gettin' to me."

He searched the floor for the other umbrella, the one with the bullets. It wasn't there. He looked back up at Batman.

And saw that his adversary held the umbrella in one gloved hand.

The Penguin took a step away. "Hey. You—wouldn't blow away an endangered bird—"

Batman raised the umbrella. He aimed straight between the Penguin's eyes.

The birdman tugged at his collar. His face was turning a very unpleasant shade of red.

He turned, and started waddling away, his breathing heavy.

"You wouldn't shoot me in the back," he called over his shoulder, "would you?"

Batman followed The Penguin with the still-raised umbrella, ready to fire.

The birdman stumbled, but started forward again, toward the last few vestiges of ice at the edge of the moat.

"I'm overheated, is all—" he gasped. "I'll murder you momentarily—"

He tugged at his collar, pulling it open.

"But first—a cool drink—"

He took a final step, then belly-flopped only a few inches from the last glistening chunk of ice at the water's edge.

"—of ice water—" he managed.

His flipper reached forward for the ice, just out of reach.

The flipper fell.

And The Penguin was still.

Batman put down the deadly umbrella. He stopped and stared as four penguins, larger than their fellows—emperor penguins, he would guess—moved forward from the shadows. They surrounded the fallen birdman, and, with a singleness of purpose, reached down with their beaks and grabbed hold of The Penguin. All four lifted their heads, raising The Penguin like pallbearers at his funeral, then turned and bore him away, back into darkness.

Batman couldn't tell anyone about this. They would never believe him.

He wasn't even sure if he believed it himself.

All the lights were on in Gotham City.

The Christmas tree blinked merrily, and the Bat signal blinked back.

Carolers sang. Children laughed. It was almost Christmas.

Commissioner Gordon sighed, and looked to the mayor and his staff. He pointed at the flashing bat emblem in the sky.

"Think he'll ever forgive us?"

The mayor shrugged. "Probably not. But he'll always help us."

Commissioner Gordon hoped so. For the sake of them all, he hoped so.

EPILOGUE

Alfred had come for him.

Battered and wounded, Bruce Wayne sat in the back of the Rolls-Royce. He stared out the window for a moment as the car passed the happy families that surrounded the tree in Gotham Plaza. But for all his hurts, and all the Christmas joy around him, he really couldn't feel anything.

"I—" he said after a while, "I didn't find her. Maybe—"

"Yes," Alfred replied. "Maybe."

Bruce looked at his butler, and his old friend. He knew, really, that Alfred didn't believe that Selina had survived; that he was only being kind to a grieving boss. Bruce had known Alfred too long to be fooled. Still, he appreciated the effort.

Alfred frowned as revelers blocked the way ahead. He turned down an alley, attempting to take a shortcut from the crowds.

"Well," Alfred continued. "Come what may. Merry Christmas, Mr. Wayne."

"Right," Bruce replied, trying somehow to return the butler's good wishes. "Sure. And 'Peace on Earth, goodwill towards men.' "

What was that?

He thought he had heard a loud "meow."

He turned to look out the back window, just in time to see a shadow dart from the street into the alley. He jumped from the still-moving car, and disappeared into the alley. He found the jet-black feline hiding amidst the cans. "Why, Miss Kitty," he thought, "what are you doing out so late?" He tucked the cat in his arms and returned to Alfred and the Rolls.

Bruce shivered as he closed the car door behind him. "Goodwill towards men," he had said?

"And women," he added.

Alfred drove on in silence.

It is late on Christmas Eve, or maybe very early Christmas morning.

High above the buildings, projected against the clouds, the signal flashes, a bright yellow oval filled with the dark shape of a bat.

It fills all the night sky, and then it is gone.

Welcome to Gotham City.